Study Guide

For Marvin Kananen's 2013 Translation of

THE CLOUD OF UNKNOWING:

Paraphrased and Comprehendible

2019

Copyright © 2019 by Marvin Kananen
All rights reserved.
1st Edition, February 2019

For permission to copy, use, or share this work or any part thereof, please contact the author.

ISBN: 9781796513714

DEDICATED
to
Kent Lutheran Church, Kent, Washington:
Pastor Jane Prestbye and the Centering Prayer
spiritual exploration group:
Anne Timlick, Cindy Hokanson, Emily Bumpous, Janice Helgeson,
Jody McCaw, Judy Nill, Lisa Kurth, Peg Hammack, and Sushila Jones.
They thought a workbook would be helpful to
better understand the book, *The Cloud of Unknowing*.
Their pastor contacted me; this "Study Guide" was written.
Without them, it would not have been done.
And to Bob McGowan, Cheryl Jurris, Jean Wahlstrom, and Jeanne Blaszczyk,
Who make me look like a more competent writer.
With love and thanks.

Cover Photo by Translator, Taizé, France

Format of the Study Guide

This Study Guide is specifically designed to be used with Marvin Kananen's 2013 translation of the anonymously written *The Cloud of Unknowing* by a 14th-century English monk. Recently Kananen transcribed it into 21st-century English, and then paraphrased it to become more comprehendible for the modern reader. Six years later this study guide was written.

Each of the 75 chapters is divided into five sections: a **Review** of the previous chapter, insight into the **Today's Reading**, nine short-answer **Questions** taken from the reading, three possible **Discussion Questions**, and a summary or added thoughts, **Final Word,** of the chapter.

A short-answer section comes from each reading. It is suggested that answers be underlined or highlighted in the textbook when an answer to the questions is found, thus making it easier to return to the answer later. Suggested answers for the questions are found at the end of this text, starting on page 82.

Discussion Questions call for caution, integrity, honesty, and openness. It is assumed you will be reading this book in a group discussion format, but it is not essential. Those in a group have the challenge of needing to trust the confidentiality of other members to never share what they hear in the group. The integrity of fellowship is a very important issue. If, however, you find yourself in a good group with people you can trust and love, the blessings will be multiplied. If you are by yourself, it is suggested you should write out your answers to the discussion questions, then reread what you have written for the previous chapter and, occasionally, reread your own words to gain insight into your growth.

This book is not meant to be simply entertaining. The monk/author wrote to a young man who was considering a religious vocation. The monk who wrote the book encouraged him to live his life dedicated to God. It wasn't the church the monk was encouraging the young man to serve; rather, it was God. As you read, may you grow in insight into yourself, into your quest for God, and into the ways of God. Be not afraid, but go forth boldly. The "**Final Word**" section is written to add insight as well as to encourage the reader to consider a commitment to a life with increased focus. It is hoped this book will help to make it the goal of life that we all serve God.

If you, as a group, try to do one chapter a week, 75 chapters would make this a 17-month journey. The book has been divided into nine sections, making it a possible two-month study, slightly less than a twenty-page study per week. Or, at the end of this book, there is a "Cheater's Section" which gives you ten chapters that can give you an overview of the book (Chapters 3, 4, 7, 15, 24, 33, 44, 53, 69, and 75). It is hoped that these chapters might give you the essence of the book. It's like seeing a sketch of a Rembrandt rather than the actual oil painting; better than nothing, maybe, but not as good. Reading it in this shortened pattern can give you only a skeleton of the book. May you hunger for more. For further reading, it is suggest you reread *The Cloud of Unknowing*, this translation and any other you find. It is the transcriber's wildest hopes that this guide might whet your appetite to repeatedly reread the entire text.

May this Study Guide serve you well. This is an atlas to lead you on your spiritual walk, a walk that will lead you to God. Travel well, my friend. Blessings to you all from the monk and the translator.

INDEX of CHAPTER TITLES

Section I: The Clouds
1. The Four Stages
2. Invitation
3. Cloud of Unknowing
4. Cloud of Darkness
5. Cloud of Forgetting

Section II: Words
6. Stay in the Cloud
7. Finding One Word
8. Active and Contemplative Lives
9. Your Mind is the Deceiver
10. Wrath, Envy, Sloth, Pride, Covetousness, Gluttony, Lechery
11. Deadly Sins
12. Meddling with Intent
13. Meekness
14. Your Wretchedness
15. Contrition, Confession, Atonement

Section III: Martha and Mary
16. Mary's Love
17. The Active Life
18. Those Who Fall Away
19. Forgiveness
20. Martha Rebuked
21. Good, Better, Best
22. For Love of Mary
23. Enough is All
24. Two Loves

Section IV: The Work
25. One Little Act of Love
26. Salvation for Others
27. Who Will Labor?
28. The Work of Salvation
29. Who is Saved?
30. Judges
31. Burying Your Thoughts
32. Cowering
33. The Burden of Original Sin

Section V: Meditations
34. One Way
35. Lessons, Meditations, and Prayers
36. Words
37. One Word
38. Height, Depth, Breadth, Length
39. The Single Word
40. Both Words
41. In Sickness and in Health
42. Self-Control

Section VI: Lessening the Self
43. Forgetting Yourself
44. Love and Sorrow
45. Falseness
46. Heed Not Your Own Heart
47. Things Kept from God
48. Thoughts
49. Perfection of Will
50. Both the Weak and Strong
51. The Lost One
52. Fallen Imagination
53. The Lost Being Lost
54. The Contemplative's Demeanor

Section VII: Directions
55. The Deceiver
56. The Deceived
57. Up
58. Standing in Heaven
59. On this Earth
60. Direction of Heaven
61. Spiritually Upright
62. God Is above You

Section VIII: Mentally Arriving
63. Mind and Body
64. Reason
65. Imagination
66. Sensuality
67. Arriving
68. Being Nothing
69. Nothingness
70. Discernment

Section IX: Example of the Three
71. Aaron's State
72. Contemplative States
73. Bezaleel's Role
74. Your Book, Only
75. A Final Word

Section I: The Clouds

The Cloud of Unknowing   CHAPTER ONE: The Four Stages (pp. 15-16)

Review: This review is based on the Introduction (pp. 3-13) of Marvin Kananen's translation of *The Cloud of Unknowing*. The 14th Century writer of this book is not known; he is simply referred to as the monk. The purpose of this Study Guide is to help clarify the author's original message and show us details that make up the book's "big picture."

Today's Reading: In this first chapter, the author offers a simplified definition that showing that everyone fits into one of four states: Common, Special, Singular, and Perfect. The anonymous monk then explains how we are invited to enter the third state of Christian living, the "Singular." His claim is that if we are reading these words, God must have invited us. I like this thinking. Welcome.

Questions: Taken from the reading, complete the following sentences with a short answer.

1. The first of the four states is called the _____.
2. The price to be in this first state was _____.
3. The second of the four states is called the _____.
4. You reached this second state because God would not _____.
5. The third of the four states is called the _____.
6. You would not be reading this book unless you _____.
7. This book we're reading holds the _____ of what you will find in the third state.
8. The fourth of the four states is called the _____.
9. Our Lord gives you the right to be called _____.

Discussion Questions:

10. This book has been notoriously difficult to appreciate because from it you are expected to know yourself better through knowing God better. Most of the world would flee from gaining either of these insights. Our first discussion question is this: **"Assuming you want to know more about yourself, who or what brought you to this point in life where you are willing to seek God?"**
11. This book does not question your salvation; it assumes anyone who would read this book knows of the Grace of Salvation. Assuming the monk, the writer of this book, were to ask you this question, "What do you seek?" **What would you say to him?**
12. This translator assumes you already know you couldn't be perfect, or a Perfect. The other three stages are part of our spiritual evolution: Common, Special, and Singular. We have all probably made that journey through the first two stages, and it is here, as Singulars, that we grow together. **Using these three stages, tell us of your journey to become a Singular.**

Final Word: To say there are only four stages is almost too simple, yet it works. The author could have said there were twelve stages, which would also have been true. What this book can do is bring you closer to God; it can help you understand yourself and your relationship with God. That relationship is real. May this journey be fruitful for you, enabling you to grow in many directions. When you get weary, read on. When you think you understand the message of the book, read on. This is not a book to be read in a weekend; it's like an atlas that we can carry with us for a time. This book recognizes you as a "Singular" and it guides you on your way.

Date: While it may not seem important now, please record the date you start this journey. It will be something you'll want to know later. The date today is:

_____

The Cloud of Unknowing   CHAPTER TWO: Invitation (pp. 17-19)

Review: Although there are four stages or states of our Christian walk, this book only considers the third level, the Singulars. The first two states, Common and Special, are levels where once we were, but we heard a call, maybe felt an urge to know more. This book covers the manner of living that holds the essence of what we seek. You are in a good place; of this you can be certain. Read on; let us find where we are headed.

Today's Reading: The title of this chapter is "Invitation." You are included, loved, welcomed, and your presence is desired. These are good words. But today's reading is also a mirror for self-examination. Could we truly be as terrible as we are told we are? Probably. But that's not the bottom line; instead it is the understanding that our sin is what opens us up to accept the love and promise that God grants us. Without that sin, there would have been no need for Jesus. Truly, this is an invitation.

Questions: Taken from the reading, complete the following sentences with a short answer.
1. Imagine this: that you _____ worthy of being called by our Lord.
2. Have you overcome that _____ the world wants you in?
3. O wretched friend, beware, for the _____.
4. You should be _____ toward God as with a spiritual spouse.
5. This is a foretaste of your heritage that is the _____.
6. Personal meekness can be found by _____.
7. The enemies of God _____.
8. Meekly seek God in your prayers and do not _____.
9. Know this: God is fully ready and _____.

Discussion Questions:
10. The image we strive to project to the world is that we "have it together" as individuals. This chapter addresses those parts of us we try to keep hidden. Did you identify with any of the characteristics of this chapter? Your vocabulary may be different but the truths aren't. It is hard when we look at ourselves and admit how far short we are from being that perfect person we want to be. **Discuss the difference between your public image and you private one, always sharing only what you feel comfortable to share.**
11. "The enemies of God are now your enemies." That is a difficult and bold statement; it feels as if we were enlisting in the army in a time of war. Jesus says to "love your enemies." Both statements are 100% true. **How do you reconcile them in your heart?**
12. Not your pastor, priest, family, friend, or spouse can answer this next question for you. Remember this is not a reading book: this is a book for your faith journey. It takes courage to seek the things of God. Thank you for having the nerve to read further in this book. **What does the monk mean when he says that God wants you here, now, reading this book?**

Final Word: It is true, we are all weak, wretched, and wounded. In this you are not unique. You are, however, uniquely weak, wretched, and wounded. This is one of the amazing qualities of God, that we may be loved for our weaknesses, probably even more than for our strengths. When Christ cried from the cross, "Why have you forsaken me?" I can imagine that almost breaking the heart of God. When we cry out, God hears, loves, and responds.

The Cloud of Unknowing   CHAPTER THREE: Cloud of Unknowing (pp. 20-21)

Review: Trying to be perfect is the whip Satan snaps at us to inflict pain, to show our many flaws, and then tempts us to hide the scars and bruises. On the other hand, God loves us through our foibles and failings. In weakness we become stronger, in surrender we find victory. God does not seem to care about our image. God loves us with a love we are not capable of understanding, but it is a love that we can believe in: this is called faith.

Today's Reading: This reading opens with eight imperatives (commands). Here are two more: "Stop! Go back and read Chapter Three again." This chapter is the essence of the book; this is why we are reading it. This is the answer to Chapter Two's final discussion suggestion. This is what we seek: to understand that we truly are evil and our only hope can be found in seeking God. This is the great Cloud of Unknowing; it's not just a name of a book but it's where God dwells. The Cloud contains all that is good and worthy. It is where God is to be found. Amen! Alleluia!

Questions: Taken from the reading, complete the following sentences with a short answer.

1. The _____ is to please God.
2. _____ will grow enraged when you do what is joyful to God.
3. Evil will try to _____, if it can.
4. Do not _____, but labor in this work.
5. Your first lesson is when you first encounter _____.
6. The Cloud will _____, between you and your God.
7. It will convince you that _____ in this wonderful darkness.
8. It is a place where you will _____ better.
9. This is proof of God's mercy _____.

Discussion Questions:
10. It says: "Lift up your heart to God!" **Describe how and why a person might do this.**
11. When we lose ourselves in working for God, it is a blessing and can leave us vulnerable, in a darkness of sorts. Have you ever so lost yourself in a task that you forgot where you were? That is what it feels like to have an encounter with the Cloud of Unknowing. **Identify times when you were lost in yourself. What were the circumstances?**
12. The darkness described could feel terrifying, yet as you become more familiar with it, you'll realize it is in that dark Cloud where you want to be. There your love for God can grow. It is in the light that we find joy, but it is in this kind of darkness we can grow and change, like a plant in winter that readies itself for spring. **Does this description trouble you? Why or why not?**

Final Word: This chapter is like getting God's address. It tells us of our life's work (to please God), to serve others, and to keep our heart and mind on God. My favorite line in this third chapter about the Cloud of Unknowing is this: "Wisely, it prevents you from seeing God clearly by the light of your own understanding or reasoning." God is not in a defensive position; we are kept from seeing because we wouldn't understand what we saw. God is beyond our logic. The purpose of that Cloud of Unknowing is to protect us, not to protect God from us.

The Cloud of Unknowing   **CHAPTER FOUR**: Cloud of Darkness (pp. 22-28)

Review: There are three clouds we are discussing: first, we looked at the Cloud of Unknowing, now we consider the Cloud of Darkness, and later we will look at the Cloud of Forgetting. The Cloud of Unknowing is what surrounds God, protecting us in this lifetime from approaching the throne of God too closely. The previous chapter implied that even if we saw God, we could not comprehend what we were seeing, that our logic would fail us.

Today's Reading: Seven pages long, this is the longest chapter in the book. It is not in the Cloud of Unknowing where we will battle evil and confront ourselves, rather; it is in this second cloud, the Cloud of Darkness. In my copy of this chapter I have two notes written to myself: "I am here because I read a book once and it melted my soul;" and, "Do not speed-read this chapter." It is in the Cloud of Darkness we dwell now. Read it again carefully to better know yourself and the world where we live.

Questions: Taken from the reading, complete the following sentences with a short answer.

1. You will be asked to _____ of how you used that time given you.
2. You will be measured in one thing: _____.
3. Not merely your willingness but it is your _____to do what is right.
4. It is only with the _____ that God grants that you can have hope.
5. Without that grace, God is _____to any of creation.
6. By this work, we may someday be considered _____.
7. Live as if you keep a good _____.
8. Don't struggle in thoughts of your _____ that only lead you to a worthless end.
9. For when I say _____, I mean the lack of knowledge.

Discussion Questions:

10. This may be the most important and emotional chapter in the book. Like the last chapter, it is recommended you read it several times. **Share what attracted your attention in your readings, pointing out words, thoughts, or reactions that you gained with your first and the following readings.**
11. In the second paragraph, and repeated later, the monk refers to the accounting of your time. Here is a proposition: Set a 30-minute timer for one day and, each time it chimed, record what you were doing. If we must someday give an account of our time to God, it would be good if we knew that answer for ourselves. **What did you learn about yourself?**
12. The middle of the 7th paragraph on page 24 reads: "We may someday be considered never to have sinned." This is not an Old Testament promise—this is from Jesus. Amen. **How does that make you feel, this super forgiveness that not only are we forgiven but that we can be considered to have never sinned?**

Final Word: Be not afraid of this chapter or the truths it contains. We are held accountable for our time, told to do what is right, informed we are weak, corrupt in the flesh, dangerous in imagination and wit, and our task is to proceed forward. Change isn't easy, but we need change if we are to grow. We just read that Darkness is the lack of knowledge; the next chapter offers us some needed relief.

The Cloud of Unknowing   CHAPTER FIVE: Cloud of Forgetting (pp. 29-30)

Review: The last chapter was rightfully named, the "Cloud of Darkness." As we emerge from that chapter, it is hoped we are more aware of our sinful nature, the unavoidability of sin in the world, and the great promise that lies ahead. None of us is alone in our sinfulness and shame, but you alone are held accountable for your own sin. To be aware of your own nature is part of the growth we are all experiencing.

Today's Reading: This Cloud of Forgetting is like a shadow that protects us from the sun, or in this case, our sin. It is a gift from God, a sheltering place that enables us to focus on God and not on ourselves as in the previous chapter. Here we will talk about turning our eyes away from the world that has so burdened us and, instead, look up to God and the things of God.

Questions: Taken from the reading, complete the following sentences with a short answer.

1. _____ will always stand between you and your God.
2. The Cloud of Forgetting separates you from _____.
3. You may think you are far from God … but God is _____.
4. Creation is not only physical creation, but all the _____ and the _____.
5. _____ is for our sake, not for theirs and not for God's sake.
6. The ways of God's creation are made, these are not _____.
7. For this current time, there is _____ between you and your God.
8. It profits you nothing to consider the _____ of God.
9. Focus upon God's pure presence, to _____ God alone.

Discussion Questions:
10. In your own words, restate what the Cloud of Forgetting does and why it needs to exist in order that we may grow. **Share your thoughts with others.**
11. This chapter says, "It profits you little or nothing to consider the kindness and the worthiness of God." These are words we'll probably never hear in church. **Why do you think the author said this? Do you think it's true? Why or why not?**
12. In the second paragraph it says: "We dare not judge any creature, whether in body or in spirit, or consider their condition as to whether in body or in spirit." Later we will talk about discernment, but for now consider the words and the spirit of these words. **How does your faith help you not to judge others or react when others judge you?**

Final Word: In this reading, the first sentence of the second paragraph holds a great truth: you may be distant from God, but God is never distant from you. We live in the middle cloud, the Cloud of Darkness. This Cloud of Forgetting is a cleansing cloud where we no longer see or live. It is a very real world of blatant sinfulness. It is our means of literally forgetting that world. On the other hand, we can't yet dwell in the Cloud of Unknowing because we are not yet fit. Thus, we are adrift between two islands. Let us row toward the shore before us and leave behind the things of the world.

Confession: Did you know the original author here speaks of only two clouds and not the Cloud of Forgetting as the third Cloud as your translator did? I ask your forgiveness and toleration for such liberties. I tried to stay true to the original text but sometimes; for clarity's sake, I changed a few words but not the message. I'd guess the monk was referring to the "two other Clouds."

Section II: Words

The Cloud of Unknowing — CHAPTER SIX: Stay in the Cloud (pp. 31-32)

Review: We have shared a quick introduction to the three clouds, one where God dwells, one where we dwell, and the third, the world we are trying to leave behind. The following ten chapters, "Section II: Words," give us tools and encourage us to develop skills to carry on with our quest to move closer to God.

Today's Reading: May I share some wisdom with you: Stay in the Cloud. People in our life will beat us down with their logic and common sense about why we should not seek God. They will take arrows to shoot at us from their quivers of fear. They will claim to want to protect us, but they are only trying to keep us at their level. It is hardest when those we love, family and best friends, try to talk "reason" to us. In truth, God is the reason you dare to grow. Stand firm and stay in the cloud.

Questions: Taken from the reading, complete the following sentences with a short answer.

1. The most common answer about God is to say: "_____."
2. _____ is where we want to reside.
3. Through grace, this is _____ where one may come to a full understanding.
4. Consider God, even as you realize _____.
5. Leave all the things _____ and instead chose to love God.
6. While God may be loved, _____.
7. God may be found by love and held by our hearts but _____.
8. Seek to pierce that _____ that is above you.
9. Do not _____, no matter what happens.

Discussion Questions:

10. Here is a phrase of honesty: "I don't know." When it comes to understanding God and the ways of God, we cannot declare that we understand God. We can believe with a full heart and not understand. This will forever be true in this lifetime. Sadly, in today's world, many of us are taught never to say, "I don't know," as if it implied ignorance. Regarding the things of God, it's the best we can do. It's OK to say, "I don't know." It's the right thing to say, especially if you don't know. Have you said those words or, maybe worse, didn't say them when it would have been better to speak the truth? **If you're willing, please relate any story when you should have said, "I don't know," instead of pretending that you did know.**
11. Much of our churchly knowledge of God is based on ancient traditions and old artwork. Be aware: nothing but the Spirit can reveal the magnificence of God to you. Imagine your favorite image of God. **What description of God makes you happiest?**
12. We find God in our heart, the center of our well being, not in our head. To believe without seeing is called faith. It varies, but how would you rate your faith on a scale of one-to-ten? By staying in the Cloud, your faith will grow. **Explain your heart-felt faith to someone who sincerely asks you.**

Final Word: My faith is my compass. My home is in the Cloud of Darkness, my past is in the Cloud of Forgetting, and my path now leads me to the Cloud of the Unknowing. I will stay in the Cloud and I will seek the way into the Cloud of Unknowing. My success is found in God's love for me. Amen

The Cloud of Unknowing   CHAPTER SEVEN: Finding One Word (pp. 33-35)

Review: There are two clouds: one is the Cloud of Forgetting where you can leave the world and its cares behind and move closer to God, and also the thick Cloud of Unknowing where God dwells. In this lifetime you will never reach God, but you can live in that Cloud of Darkness and not cease serving God, no matter what happens.

Today's Reading: Chapter Seven is a chapter on self-defense. Too often we are our own worst enemies; this chapter points out some of the ways we distract ourselves with questions, thoughts, and feelings that keep us from focusing upon that which is the most important. The solution is wonderfully simple. Have a word or short phrase that you can use as an amulet or mantra to bring your mind back to what really matters—God!

Questions: Taken from the reading, complete the following sentences with a short answer.

1. What do you seek? You must simply say, "_____."
2. From the beginning, _____ that God is sweet and loving.
3. Evil does not always lie, _____.
4. _____ will babble more and more until they bring you far from God's passion.
5. If you listen to these thoughts willingly, you have left God behind _____.
6. Your thoughts ought to be buried under the _____.
7. Seek God without _____ other than finding and serving God.
8. It would be wise if you can contain this desire in a _____.
9. If intruding thoughts offer to give you insight into your chosen word, do not _____.

Discussion Questions:

10. In the third paragraph there is a warning of how enthusiastic and wonderful our thoughts may seem regarding our goals and purpose, thoughts that assure us that God is sweet, full of grace, and merciful. To prevent us from listening or believing ourselves is not an easy thing to do. **What criteria do you use to discern the truths of what we say or think to ourselves?**
11. A mantra is a 3,000 year-old Sanskrit word defined as a sound repeated to aid concentration in meditation, which this chapter suggests we find. Later, Buddhists and Hindus used it, but do not let that hinder you. Find a word that will keep your mind on God. Although it may change in time, always choose a word that keeps your thoughts on God. **Share the word that you are inclined to use.**
12. A mantra's design is to keep our distracting thoughts from stealing our focus. Often these distractions have their source in evil. The book will not help us here. **Now would be a good place to discuss what "evil" is today and what thoughts distract you as you try to meditate.**

Final Word: This chapter could affect you for the rest of your life. When I walk, I repeat short phrases. If I say "Jesus Christ" I take three steps (three syllables) and remain silent on the fourth step, then I repeat it. If I say "God" I say it and then take three steps in silence, then repeat it. I think of it as a brain cleansing. Try it.

The Cloud of Unknowing   CHAPTER EIGHT: Active and Contemplative Lives (pp. 36-40)

Review: I hope you found your "one word" from Chapter Seven. It may work to stay with your first word, but don't randomly choose this word. Try other words, some feel good about their word but the feeling soon fades; others start slowly but catch on. I say "Lord" more often than I say the name "God" because, when I use the latter word, I can feel the weight of that word in my heart. I am in awe of God; sometimes I hesitate to call him by that name too casually. In cheerful moods, I often say "Adonai" (LORD) and it almost makes me want to skip along to that three-syllable, three-step word. Try other words, and when you find one word or phrase that you feel most deeply, cling to it.

Today's Reading: Three of the first four sentences in Chapter 8 are questions aimed at helping us realize that the Cloud of Forgetting is there to protect us, especially from ourselves. It is not until the fifth paragraph that we approach the real subject of this chapter, the difference between the Active and Contemplative lifestyles.

Questions: Taken from the reading, complete the following sentences with a short answer.
1. About now you should be asking, "Who _____?"
2. _____ causes you to swell with pride and with curiosity.
3. This _____ when earnest scholars strive to become masters of vanity.
4. The two degrees of both Active and Contemplative lives are _____ & _____.
5. The lower part of the Active Life does the real works of _____ and _____.
6. In the higher part of the Contemplative Life, one is _____.
7. Words done in the Darkness are _____.
8. It is _____ we may be able to reach God in this life, but never with knowledge.
9. Our good and noble-seeming thoughts actually lead us into _____.

Discussion Questions:
10. The Cloud of Forgetting is a dynamic gift from God. It is part of the Grace that God gives us. It frees us to change our focus and ever seek the higher things. The world and the people of the world, often your family members, are willing to remind you of the "good" things you're leaving behind. There are some things we can say to them (and, at times, to ourselves) to quiet them. **There is power that is found in accepting the Cloud of Forgetting in our lives. In what ways do we recognize this power?**
11. The monk considers the higher Active similar to, but not the same as, a lower Contemplative. Sometimes the difference is not discernible. The work is not always physical work; sometimes the goals of the Contemplative are truly different than the Active's purposes. Think here of Mother (now Saint) Teresa and her roles throughout her life.. **Together, discuss what might be some of the goals of the Contemplative.**
12. When I became a missionary, I hoped to be a higher Contemplative, but life in Africa made me an Active. I wanted to be a Mary but the situation forced me to become a Martha. **Describe any situations that may have caused you to be a doer (Active) instead of a student (Contemplative).**

Final Word: Do not seek to find humility in your past; rather examine yourself as you are at this moment in your current state. Then you may begin to understand wretchedness. This is not the modern way to examine yourself, but it is God's way and it is truth's way.

The Cloud of Unknowing   CHAPTER NINE: Your Mind is a Deceiver (pp. 41-43)

Review: Chapter 8 spoke of the differences and similarities between the Actives and the Contemplatives. All four states of the two classes are good and honorable. The lesson was to remind us to keep our hearts and minds on things that are truly of God and not to allow ourselves to be misled either by the devil or, more often, by ourselves.

Today's Reading: The intent of Chapter 9 is to constantly remind us that we will always be tempted, no matter which course we take. It is not merely the devil or others who will try to lead us away from the path to God, but we do it to ourselves with cunningly devised and self-inflicted excuses. Not all our thoughts are evil, but enough are so that we always have to be careful. Our goal is not to be found in vanity, but in the peace God alone can provide.

Questions: Taken from the reading, complete the following sentences with a short answer.

1. You will find yourself continually tempted from _____ whenever you do good.
2. You need to be aware that _____ is not clean, but of thoughts other than God.
3. This is often the truth: _____ thoughts will prove to be profitable to your soul.
4. The love of God is a _____ by which you will know the Cloud of Unknowing better.
5. _____ are open in contemplation that you can witness the angels and saints.
6. Many who seek to see the things of God fall short, victim of their own _____.
7. Everything your mind imagines will _____ in your purpose?
8. Not all thoughts are _____. May God keep you from misinterpreting your thoughts.
9. Do not seek peace of mind through saints or angels, but seek your peace _____.

Discussion Questions:
10. With every new and righteous work come new disappointments, temptations, and hurdles that seem intent on discouraging us. Sometimes it's easiest to do nothing, but doing nothing is not always right, either. We all have examples where doing what was good and right became more difficult. **Please share an example with the group**.
11. The text reads, "Not all thoughts are evil" (paragraph 5). That sentence implies that some, maybe most, of our thoughts are not God-directed. **How can we discern which of our thoughts are wrong, evil, or misleading as opposed to what is right and pure?**
12. There is a promise of a very deep and private love by which you will finally begin to know the Cloud of Unknowing better. It is a thought the world would not understand. **Why does or why doesn't that thought bring you comfort?**

Final Word: The way to God is a maze; our feelings can mislead us, as can our thoughts, friends, and hunches, not to mention devilish temptations and vanity. Yet the way is not impossible; it is merely difficult. The route to God is not a sprint, it is taken at a slowly measured pace during which everything is questioned, nothing is certain. It is only our God-given faith that provides us with the will and strength to continue along the right path.

The Cloud of Unknowing   CHAPTER TEN: Wrath, Envy, Sloth, Pride, etc. (pp. 44-45)

Review: If we can't trust ourselves, who can we trust? God. It's sometimes easy to convince ourselves we are born without sin, but it's not true. We tell ourselves many things we want to be true, even when we know they aren't. We choose to believe the falsehood and thereby deceive ourselves. We wish we were better, taller, younger, lighter, prettier, smarter, but we are as we are. That's hard to accept. Almost always, the lie is more pleasant than the truth. Chapter Nine offered us this advice: Resist the pressures from your will and thinking; trust only God. Then you do well.

Today's Reading: The "Seven Deadly Sins" are not directly biblical. They have been a part of the Catholic teachings since the Fourth-Century monk, Evagrius Ponticus, and were later enumerated (numbered) by Pope Gregory I. These are not necessarily "deadly" sins, nor are they a complete list of our innate sins, but they are reminders that our hearts and minds are frail and need to be restrained.

Questions: Taken from the reading, complete the following sentences with a short answer.

1. Seek peace in God and not what those of the world _____.
2. Our thoughts may lead us to believe _____ can be attributed to you.
3. For your heart is _____ and needs to be _____.
4. Your sins, whether private or public, religious or secular, are _____ sins.
5. Resentment in your heart, if uncorrected, will fasten to your _____.
6. What is the passion with an appetite for vengeance? It is _____.
7. A state of listlessness of good works may be called _____.
8. Of the 7 "deadly sins," _____ is the only one mentioned in the Ten Commandments.
9. Dalliance, cajoling, and flattering that seem innocent are really forms of _____.

Discussion Questions:

10. Some of these sins seem more offensive than others. Certainly there are others we could list as well. In this current age there are sins that were not imagined two thousand years ago, and yet, sin is sin is sin. **Discuss whether you think we are worse sinners today than we were when Pope Gregory limited the number of deadly sins to seven.**
11. Two of the words, covetousness and envy, seem very similar; yet they are different. **What would you say is the difference between envy and covetousness?**
12. Imagine that you had the opportunity to replace any or all of the "seven deadly sins." **Which of these sins would you replace and which would you leave on the list: wrath, envy, sloth, pride, covetousness, gluttony, and lechery?**

Final Word: These seven sins often hide themselves in other passions. I think of the young man completely enrapt in playing electronic games who, I suspected, was hiding his slothfulness. Examine your life for similar things like gluttony hidden in dieting, lechery in pornography, etc. Discuss this with no one, but examine yourself with this sure knowledge that we are all sinners, whether overt or covert. When our sins are forgiven, they are truly forgiven. This truth is one of the elements in recognizing our own wretchedness.

The Cloud of Unknowing   CHAPTER ELEVEN: Deadly Sins (pp. 46-47)

Review: The Fourth Century Catholic Church formulated a list of eight words that loosely summed up the sins of the human race. Several hundred years later, Pope Gregory I (the Great) reduced the number to seven. Interestingly, the word "despond" was dropped from the list, probably to make the number of sins a divine number—seven. Despond meant to be dejected or to be in low spirits; it was once upon a time considered a "deadly sin."

Today's Reading: Chapter Eleven is only 165 words long. It is the antidote for Chapter Ten. It gives the serum that can neutralize the poison of the "deadly sins." A chapter of hope, it provides an answer to the sins of the world. Most importantly, it says the above-mentioned sins are forgivable.

Questions: Taken from the reading, complete the following sentences with a short answer.

1. You need to consider each _____ and every _____ you find stirring within you.
2. Those who seek to be closer to God will _____ with some of these things.
3. Consider the thoughts you are _____, not in order to sin, but not to sin.
4. Even if you do not take hold of the first thought, you cannot avoid the _____.
5. Forgivable sins cannot be _____ in this deadly life.
6. Though these sins are forgivable, they should be avoided by _____.
7. _____ in those sins, though they are forgivable, should always be avoided.
8. Be a disciple of our Lord's _____.
9. Do not be surprised when others _____ to deadly sins.

Discussion Questions:

10. Discuss the following thought: **If sin is always sin, are there degrees of sin, as if some sins are worse than others?**
11. Murder is not mentioned in this list, probably because it is something we don't all do, yet it certainly seems it should be classified as a "deadly" sin. **Were it up to us, what would we classify as a "deadly" sin?**
12. If sin is so bad, how difficult would it be for us to simply avoid these sins from now on? **Discuss.**

Final Word: Without baptism, without faith, and without trust in God, there is no other way that we sinners can hope for forgiveness. We who have these three things are truly a richly blessed people. But those without the understanding to realize that all are sinners and fall short of perfection cannot comprehend our source of hope. The following chapters intend to remind us that the path we walk is not broad and easy, and that we will be held accountable for our progress. Leave behind what is deadly and move further into the great hope of the Cloud of Unknowing where dwells our God.

The Cloud of Unknowing   CHAPTER TWELVE: Meddling with Intent (pp. 48-49)

Review: Sometimes perfection is held up as the right and desired way to be, but in truth we are thoroughly sinners in a sinful world. However, we don't have to be a part of the world. By knowing ourselves, we can move to an area where we can live among the sin but not indulge in it. We've covered a range of behaviors to avoid, but remember, our goal is higher than that—to dwell in the Cloud of Unknowing. Let us strive together in that journey.

Today's Reading: Chapter Twelve's title, "Meddling with Intent," comes from the fourth paragraph in today's reading. The actual quotation is "… being without any meddling of vain intent." It is a warning! It tells us that our virtues can become tainted with sin if our intentions are crooked or imperfect. This chapter's intent is to keep us on the path that leads to God and warns us about varying from the course.

Questions: Taken from the reading, complete the following sentences with a short answer.

1. Stand with love and do not fall, never _____ in your purpose.
2. _____ in this Cloud of Unknowing that lies between you and God.
3. Do not go where _____, for this is where sin works.
4. Despite all you do, there will still remain in you the _____ of sin.
5. Nothing can be done without this _____.
6. Those without the heart stirring will profit _____.
7. _____ is an ordered and a measured affection that is directed towards God.
8. Assume there are two major virtues: _____.
9. With these virtues it would seem enough to have it all. But, _____.

Discussion Questions:

10. The first four words of paragraph two: "If you must hate…" does not mean you must hate, yet some of us find our passion in a state of outrage. To hate that which is evil, that is anything that does not serve God, is not a deadly sin. Advice: Hate the sin, not the sinner. **Give a few examples where you can imagine a "righteous hatred."**
11. Same paragraph, second sentence: "Do not go where evil things lurk." That is obviously true, yet our vanity may instill within us the need to return to the site of former evils while claiming we do so for the sake of others. It is a trap our flesh may too willingly enter eagerly. **Identify situations where it might be best for reforming sinners to avoid**.
12. This chapter ends with a sudden slamming of a door. After apparently singing the praises of Meekness and Charity, the last sentence says, "They do not." These wonderful virtues are not enough. **Discuss why these two virtues may not be adequate.**

Final Word: The message in Chapter Twelve comes in the fourth paragraph: it speaks of experiencing a heart that has been stirred by God. This heart-stirring is the source of our energy and courage. It carries us to places that others cannot see, face, or go. The stirring of your heart is a gift of God; it marks the presence of the Holy Spirit within you. Without it you may have some success, but the author wants you to earnestly pursue that stirring which only God can provide.

The Cloud of Unknowing   CHAPTER THIRTEEN: Meekness (pp. 50-51)

Review: The closing words of Chapter Twelve warned us that the two wonderful virtues of Meekness and Charity, although seemingly wonderful, are inadequate without a spiritual stirring of the heart. Here we address only the major virtue of meekness. It is good to do so.

Today's Reading: Meekness is a virtue often seen as an image of humility. Sometimes it is exactly what it appears to be, a God-inspired sense of awe mixed with our own sense of unworthiness. As good as we can be, the best we can do falls far short of the perfection of God. However, by the presence of God, our meekness is free to blossom. We receive that quality that only God can grant and which the Holy Spirit can then utilize.

Questions: Taken from the reading, complete the following sentences with a short answer.

1. Meekness is imperfect unless it is caused by _____.
2. Meekness is nothing more than the _____ and feeling of one's self-worth.
3. Meekness is the realization of the _____, _____ and _____ of the human race.
4. Meekness is the recognition of the _____ of God.
5. We ought to quake and tremble in comparison to _____.
6. Realize that in comparison to God's perfection, without end, all else is _____.
7. The abundance of God's grace in our life has been multiplied by _____.
8. There is only one cause for change, the source of this change is _____.
9. May God _____ from seeking this grace by any other means.

Discussion Questions:

10. Ask yourself if you know anyone who you consider to be meek. **What are the qualities that cause you to label that person as meek?**
11. The two causes of meekness are said to be wretchedness and love, two very opposite states. **Discuss this apparent contradiction and how you reconcile these opposites.**
12. One of the proofs of the existence of the Cloud of Forgetting is how completely we can forget the sins of our past, unable even to recall what we've forgotten. Sometimes we are reminded of something we did by someone else and we cannot remember what is being spoken of. If you think that isn't true, ask an older sibling. Neither they nor we can grant us forgiveness or forgetfulness; only God can grant those gifts. **Compare your understanding of meekness with the author's.**

Final Word: Meekness is not an image; it is a state of being. It is not a condition we can claim as a result of our own doing or behavior; true meekness has one source—God! To claim otherwise is slanderous. Be blind to your own meekness and servant heart; do what is good and right in the sight of God.

The Cloud of Unknowing   **CHAPTER FOURTEEN**: Your Wretchedness (pp. 52-53)

Review: The parents of Meekness are Imperfection and Awe. There is no compromise. There is only the searching for God's perfection and the realization that we are not worthy to seek God, which is then proof that we are. It is a knot that we cannot untie; meekness is an answer to a question that cannot be asked. Seek and serve God, then you will know.

Today's Reading: With infinite wisdom, God neither gives us more trials than we can bear nor more knowledge than we can handle. One of the great truths of creation is that we can never be truly meek until we realize that we cannot be meek and know it. This is the knowledge we can grasp from our unworthiness and wretchedness. It is not until we realize our failings and shortcomings that we can be meek, but then it is too late. It is like being ugly until grace fills us, but when we see our reflection we only see the old ugliness while God sees the beauty in us. It is too simple for us to understand and too wonderful to deny, but it's something we need to accept without reservation.

Questions: Taken from the reading, complete the following sentences with a short answer.

1. It is impossible for sinners to find _____ if they think they gained it themselves.
2. Without the perfect virtue of meekness, _____ will never be revealed.
3. Even the meekest soul must still live in this sinful world with our _____.
4. You must leave the toil of seeking meekness and find a way of _____.
5. In body or in spirit, one can barely understand what can be done by _____.
6. This is how a pure love can be made clean in _____.
7. Not knowing what perfect meekness was, we could imagine we have _____.
8. Don't deceive yourself to imagine we are meek while still wrapped in our _____.
9. As we struggle to attain meekness, we are less likely to sin _____.

Discussion Questions:

10. From the human side, our vanity tries to persuade us that we are meek. The view is made possible by our lack of knowledge and minimalist thinking. If only for a moment, all of us probably experienced thinking we were good or acted meekly only to have the truth expose us. **If willing, relate a moment of awakening when your lack of meekness was exposed**.
11. It's true the key to meekness is wretchedness and your wretchedness is revealed only by truth and knowledge. **Explain why we should think meekness is still a blessing.**
12. The concluding paragraph is interesting. It says that if we have meekness we will sin—but not as much or as deeply. The explanation is that we will be better than we were (true), but until the Grace of God intervenes, we are far from perfect. Giving support for your answer, share your thoughts to the following question. **Does this mean sin is not as sinful if the sinner is meek?**

Final Word: Worse than feeling wretched is to feel that we are not wretched. Worst is to think we are meek when those around us know otherwise. Perhaps best is to wonder what people are speaking of when they call us meek. Finally, just serve and let meekness be an unseen shadow that follows us, as God wills it.

The Cloud of Unknowing CHAPTER FIFTEEN: Contrition, Confession, Atonement (pp. 54-55)

Review: As we finish this chapter, we finish the second section of this book called "Words." These ten chapters have given definition and application to concepts that will follow us through the rest of the book, from our special word for meditation to words that define our being. Whatever the word chosen, the two consistent themes have been that God is God and we are base sinners. Our most meaningful purpose is to reach toward God in that unfathomable Cloud of Unknowing.

Today's Reading: Chapter 15 is a graduation, of sorts. After you come to understand who and what we are and how monstrously inadequate we are, what can we do? The author offers three consecutive concepts: Contrition, Confession, and Atonement. This is another chapter worth rereading.

Questions: Taken from the reading, complete the following sentences with a short answer.

1. Seek the spirit of meekness that may come to you through _____ in this lifetime.
2. With time the _____ of our sins will be rubbed away as our conscience grows.
3. Some claim they have maintained some _____ and never willfully sinned.
4. Our conscience bears witness of change through _____ , _____ and _____ .
5. These three acts are done in accordance with the _____ .
6. Those who feel called by _____ to become Contemplatives.
7. They who seek God know that God has already _____ .
8. Those who don't know themselves can't understand the wretchedness _____ .
9. Those who seek God will find God lives in the _____ .

Discussion Questions:

10. Some claim a degree of innocence and grace in their lives and life styles while others say sin is sin and demand judgment with vengeance. These two thoughts seem opposite and not to be resolved; yet, somehow, both may be true. **How can we reconcile this contradiction?**
11. The three steps to cause change in our lives are Contrition, Confession, and Atonement. This is not simply feeling bad and apologizing: Contrition is deep regret, Confession is the admitting of wrongdoing, and Atonement is the change that improves our lives. These are not merely religious terms; they will make our lives better in all avenues. These are on-going activities we must repeat frequently. **When is the last time you consciously felt contrite, confessed, and atoned for something you said or did? What caused or motivated it?**
12. Speaking of Jesus, our book says: "Those who seek Him find Him in the Gospels." The Bible is where we find God. *The Cloud of Unknowing* is based on the Bible. We should read the Bible often, thoroughly, deeply, slowly and with consideration. It's obvious our monk lived in the Gospel stories. We're going to spend the next 60 lessons in the Bible. No one reads the Bible "too much." **How can we give the Bible more attention in our lives?**

Final Word: Meekness is merely impossible. Impossible should never stop us, so long as it is right. Yet, if we do what is right without having to think about what is right and good, meekness happens. Apparently, when it happens, we deny it. With Contrition, Confession and Atonement as part of our lives, miracles can happen. Just do it, be it, act it, and, with God's help, it may happen. Faith comes before deep meekness can occur.

Section III: Martha and Mary:

The Cloud of Unknowing   CHAPTER SIXTEEN: Mary's Love (56-58)

Review: Chapter 15 was a trip planner. It started with the need in our lives for Contrition, Confession, and Atonement, things we must pack for the journey and things to use during pilgrimage. Eventually we come to the temporary destination of Meekness, a place we may not recognize or know when we have arrived. Using the Bible as our guide, it's in Meekness we'll find a new life. Though still in the Cloud of Darkness, we'll barely notice it. Bon Voyage!

Today's Reading: Beginning here, the next nine chapters involve applying a practical story from the Bible to our lives. The roles of two sisters, Martha and Mary, provide a significant setting in which to examine our own lives. This chapter focuses on Mary as a Contemplative. She has chosen a different spiritual path than her sister. It is good to not yet judge which of the two has chosen the better way. Read and see Mary in a new light.

Questions: Taken from the reading, complete the following sentences with a short answer.
1. _____ tell you it is presumptive for you to wish to become a Contemplative.
2. As He did to Mary, our Lord spoke to all sinners, saying, "Your sins _____."
3. The words (of forgiveness) were spoken because _____.
4. Great sorrow and weeping for one's own sins are part of the _____.
5. As with all sinners, it was _____ when she and sin were bound together.
6. Her (Mary's) sins made a _____ and her God.
7. She could never bring her own _____ to an end.
8. She had the courage to hang her love and her burning desire in this _____.
9. She saw God without regard to sin, _____.

Discussion Questions:
10. As has been said and as we know, behaviors that move us closer to God can offend many. People may say to you, "You can't do that! Not you!" This can be said in a thousand insulting ways, spoken or not. Throughout our lives, we have encountered many of these attacks; most are minor but some scar us for life. People who don't understand what we're doing seem too willing to judge us. **As Christians, how should we respond to such angry judgments?**
11. Mary was undoubtedly a sinner. It says clearly in this reading that sin causes a rift between God and us. To bridge that gap, in the last chapter we read of a three-step action that can enable us to reach out for the grace of God. **Name the three steps.**
12. In one of the great illustrations of true love, the chapter concludes with Mary and Jesus looking at each other, unaware of the other as physical or spiritual beings. They looked at each other in love, as God would have us all be. **What can we learn from their relationship?**

Final Word: Let us continue on with an assumption of the monk, the original writer, that Mary the sister of Martha is the same Mary (Magdalena) who Christ granted forgiveness for all her sins as she anointed his hair and feet with expensive oils. It's OK; some scholars say they are not the same, others say they are. Be at peace. Let us simply rejoice for all of these Marys and Marthas in our lives.

The Cloud of Unknowing   CHAPTER SEVENTEEN: The Active Life (59-60)

Review: Chapter 16 dealt with the person of Mary, a female disciple of Jesus and someone who desired to be a Contemplative, much to the dismay of her sister. Like all of us, she was a sinner since the moment of her birth but found grace for her soul. She loved Jesus completely, without regard for herself. To be a Mary is a blessed thing.

Today's Reading: Chapter 17 is the key chapter in this current section of the book. Here the author focuses on that well-known story of the two sisters, Martha and Mary, portraying them as an Active and a Contemplative. There is an innate conflict about the spiritual styles and values in this story; basically one does what needs to be done and the other seeks to understand. To Mary, knowledge is more important than work to meet the needs of others.

Questions: Taken from the reading, complete the following sentences with a short answer.

1. Martha's work was _____, the first part of the Active life.
2. Mary is in both the second part of _____ and the first part of the _____.
3. The wisdom of God remains wrapped _____ for us to understand.
4. Mary sat still in a _____ of love that lifted her into that high Cloud.
5. Mary was totally ravished by the _____ of God.
6. Martha felt she was _____ while Mary sat still and did not answer her.
7. Mary had found _____ which Martha could not understand.
8. This story is the key as an example of all _____.
9. _____ understand Mary while _____ understand Martha.

Discussion Questions:

10. Both Martha and Mary were at the third stage, the "Singular" level (see p. 16). Martha's work is "good and holy" as an Active. Too often women find themselves stuck in this position. Mary is a "lower Contemplative." They are equals, yet their roles are often very different. **Talk about the fairness of this situation, where equals are not always equal.**
11. Taking it personally, Martha thought Mary was being unkind to her and hoped Jesus would judge and rule on Martha's behalf. Jesus saw both women as doing equally important work and told Martha to leave Mary alone. **If you have a story in your life that replayed the Martha/Mary conflict, please share with the group.**
12. This story of these sisters is a key to understanding conflict in the church, especially between Contemplatives and Actives. In life and in church, there are many different roles, each being necessary and profitable for all. **Are you content with your role as you see yourself and, if not, what would you like to change?**

Final Word: As I mentioned previously, I thought I'd be a Contemplative when I went to Africa as a missionary and turned out to be 95% an Active. I was a Martha when I wanted to be a Mary, yet I have no doubt my impact on my students and the church was far greater for my role as a Martha. They are two very different roles, yet gender generally seems a deciding factor as far as social expectations go. Chapter 16 ended with a male and a female loving without regard to things bodily or spiritual, but just as they were. We should strive to be more like that, as is illustrated in the Gospel of Luke.

The Cloud of Unknowing   CHAPTER EIGHTEEN: Those Who Fall Away (61-62)

Review: The loving conflict between Martha and Mary is lived out daily in our lives. Which one is right? They both are. Is it fair? Is it right? The opportunities to serve and to grow vary daily. When you can, be a Contemplative. When you must, be an Active. Life does not always give clear-cut answers. Life is like an avalanche we can only ride; we don't steer it.

Today's Reading: Complaints and conflict, we all have too many of both in our lives. An unheeded complaint can lead to conflict. Sometimes, when we are wronged or hurt or insulted, seldom is recourse offered us. It is then we surrender to the situation, forgive, and move on. This chapter is focused on those who could not get their way in conflict, who chose not to forgive, chose not to go on, and so ended up unsatisfied and unhappy.

Questions: Taken from the reading, complete the following sentences with a short answer.

1. As with Martha's complaints, _____ complain about Contemplatives.
2. If one can live the Contemplative life with a pure conscience, _____.
3. Many have fallen from their chosen path because of _____ against them.
4. Those who complain try to make everyone lead the _____ as they once led.
5. Many people have fallen away from this path even after they chose to _____.
6. They refused to obey God in _____, becoming the devil's servants.
7. They have, in turn, led others to become similar _____.
8. Of these we choose to _____.
9. Until then, _____, but let us continue with our matter.

Discussion Questions:

10. Actives (who think they do ALL of the work) often complain about Contemplatives because this latter group may appear to be slothful. Actives may try to shame and embarrass the Contemplatives into returning to "real" work as they used to do. But Contemplatives have moved on to a new phase. **What would you say in defense of the Contemplatives?**
11. A Contemplative who returns to the world often tries to sour the faith walk of other Contemplatives. In their falling away from God's service, they think they will feel better if others join them. **If someone insisted you were on that wrong path, a way that they'd rejected, how might you handle it?**
12. This is a sad problem: That the Contemplative who turns away from God should be ignored and forgotten by other Contemplatives. This is a harsh judgment, but it is also wise. **Because it's a spiritual issue, how would you ignore those who turned away from you?**

Final Word: This is a hard chapter. Many fear change more than anything, and if they try to change and it does not immediately go well, they are quick to return to their old way. We need to let them go. We cannot allow others to stifle our walk with God. As for Actives, they really need to support Contemplatives. Protect yourself. Protect one another.

The Cloud of Unknowing   CHAPTER NINETEEN: Forgiveness (63-64)

Review: Chapter 18 was cold reality. Sadly, for those who once walked with us and then turned away, they do evil for their own selfish reasons. They'd keep us from our quest. To journey to God, often we must go alone, for such is the way to God. For some in our past, it is necessary to forget them and not to speak of them as we continue on our way toward God.

Today's Reading: In Chapter 18, the writer implied the way of the Contemplative was superior to the Active way. This chapter makes some amends. The text says "nothing is wrong with Martha," "no disrespect meant," "servant of God," "courteous and brief," etc. In truth, both roles are necessary, each with its own blessings. Martha complained to Jesus, but I suppose we all do in various ways. We are all Marthas just as we are all Marys at times.

Questions: Taken from the reading, complete the following sentences with a short answer.

1. There is nothing wrong with Martha; in fact she is a _____.
2. Truly, _____ is directed at either sister.
3. Martha should be fully excused for her complaint, considering _____.
4. Her _____ was the real cause of her misconception.
5. It is no surprise she could not recognize how _____.
6. People today know little of what it means to be a _____.
7. The world _____ why any would seek to become God's servant.
8. There is need for all who toil to pause and consider their _____.
9. _____ in that God can forgive us all for our ignorant faults.

Discussion Questions:

10. Martha was not wrong! She did not understand although she was polite about it. We'll never know if Martha ever understood or if she continued to bear a grudge. **What would you say to Martha to encourage her?**
11. The world cannot understand why anyone would give away one's life to be a servant of God. Yet we know the calling of God is magnetic for those who seek to know God. **In reading, have you felt as if you are earnestly seeking God? Share your thoughts.**
12. This translator never felt the monk/author truly made amends to the great many Actives in the world with his weak, semi-apologetic remarks. The world and those of faith need Actives to demonstrate the Gospel of Christ to the world. **Explain why you agree or disagree with the translator?**

Final Word: Truly, after chapter 18, I believe an apology was due. But as in most of life, we don't get the recognition or the apology. This is the reason for the chapter's title: "Forgiveness." I think Actives forgive the world and Contemplatives more than the Contemplatives do. Did you notice in the previous chapter it was the Contemplative who walked away from the vow, not the Active? This shows a great lesson for all of us. Let us forgive, accept, apologize, and continue on with our work as servant of God and not let the things of the world and petty minds hinder us.

The Cloud of Unknowing   CHAPTER TWENTY: Martha Rebuked (65-66)

Review: Chapter 19 began "There was nothing wrong with Martha." Mary sought more of the spiritual things of God whereas Martha, as an Active, served the physical needs as they arose. Neither Active nor Contemplative is perfect, all come short of what they ought to be. The answer lies in the Contrition, Confession, and Atonement found in Chapter 15. We are as we are; may we be forgiven our faults and shortcomings.

Today's Reading: Chapter 20 is a reminder that in this world, we all need forgiveness: we all sin and whine when we should be rejoicing. This chapter is a bit of rebuke and correction to all that has gone on before us in previous chapters.

Questions: Taken from the reading, complete the following sentences with a short answer.

1. Beginning Contemplatives _____ the Actives for their complaining.
2. Martha behaved as if her sister was _____.
3. Martha turned to Jesus to be the judge and tell Mary _____.
4. Martha wanted her brand of _____, but He defended Mary.
5. Saying, "_____," He wanted her to stop and truly listen to Him.
6. Actives always seem busy and troubled by _____ of many things.
7. Jesus told her that God _____ for God's self.
8. She could serve God imperfectly, but _____ as she may have envisioned.
9. For all love is _____.

Discussion Questions:

10. One of the communication difficulties is when someone is so busy they hear a request but do not acknowledge it, they continue with what they are doing. This is what Mary did with Martha. Mary was in a "Do Not Disturb" mood. We don't speak to a doctor in the middle of brain surgery or talk to a mechanic lining up a new transmission. Neither do you disturb someone at the blessed feet of Jesus. It wasn't a question of right or wrong, fair vs. unfair; it's about priorities. It may have happened to you; you may have done it to others. **Recall and share some of those incidents.**
11. The Active often sees life as a series of things that must be done. They judge the world on what is being accomplished. They are "busy and troubled by the multitude of details" which they are expected to do. Jesus spoke to her and said she was doing well, right, and good by God. Yet apparently Martha's feelings were hurt; she felt rebuked. The two sisters were in opposite modes. **If you were one of them, what would you say to your sister the next day?**
12. Earlier we spoke of the line "sin is sin" and acknowledged it was a true oversimplification. The last line in this chapter reads, "All love is but one love." **Is that true? Discuss this statement.**

Final Word: Active vs. Contemplative: in the mission field, one line often repeated was that we'd trade five theologians for one mechanic. Feel free to read that line as one Active for five Contemplatives. There is one God, one love, and one hope. Rejoice in that simple and deep truth.

The Cloud of Unknowing CHAPTER TWENTY-ONE: Good, Better, Best (67-69)

Review: Jesus himself recognized the difference in the roles of Actives and Contemplatives. This definition is drawn from His "Martha, Martha" advice in which He encouraged Martha that the role she'd chosen for herself was good and profitable for her soul's growth, He said of Mary that she had chosen the better role. This leads us directly into today's reading.

Today's Reading: Good, better, and best are words of judgment. Sometimes the difference is difficult to discern; at other times the way to understand is to move further back from your subject and see the "big picture." Simply put, in this application, to know Christ and to dwell above the Cloud of Forgetting is Good. Better is what Martha chose in serving God through her role as an Active. Mary's role as a Contemplative was best, to be sitting at the feet of Jesus, unmindful of the world. Martha served while Mary loved (See Luke 10:38-42).

Questions: Taken from the reading, complete the following sentences with a short answer.

1. Best is the third number in the order; there is no _____.
2. In these two lifestyles, there are _____.
3. The first part stands for good and honest physical works of _____.
4. Good spiritual meditations consider _____ , _____ , & _____ .
5. Actives may come to _____, but no higher.
6. To possess the most pure love for God, _____ puts them there.
7. _____ are both good and holy, yet they end in this life.
8. The _____ shall never be taken away; …, it will continue forever.
9. _____ with those who have chosen to be Contemplatives.

Discussion Questions:

10. With thanks to BibleGateway.com, I looked at the word used to describe Mary's choice in Luke 10:42. Translators chose "best" in 11% of the Bibles, 62% chose "good" or "better." All 45 translations are defendable in their word choice for the Greek *agathos* (αγαθην), generally translated as "good." **How would you describe Mary's choice? Why?**

11. Actives and Contemplatives may never agree on what is right. Actives generally cannot understand a Contemplative, nor can the Contemplative understand why the Active doesn't strive to be a Contemplative. As Jesus said, "Both are good." Yet even the strongest Contemplative, if working with kids, soon becomes a Martha-like Active for a time. It happens because our work is to do what needs to be done. If Actives teach a Bible Class for a short time, they are Contemplatives. **In your life, have you had a situation where you move from one such role to another?**

12. Words of praise to the Active are deserved and thanks go to Contemplatives. Neither is right or wrong in terms of the other, "Best" applies rarely. Often we don't choose our roles; we simply do what is right. Seldom do we get the "best" of anything, more often it is forms of "good enough" we get. **If you have one, please share a "best" experience when others affirmed your new role.**

Final Word: Legalists probably wish for words like gooder, betterer and bestest to further judge others by finite, petty degrees. It is better that we don't judge on such qualitative scales.

The Cloud of Unknowing   CHAPTER TWENTY-TWO: For Love of Mary (70-71)

Review: The last chapter was terribly subjective and judgmental. Do not get bogged down in the minutiae, but keep your heart and mind on God. To both love and serve God is best.

Today's Reading: Chapter 22 is a love story. It tries to explain Mary's complete, single-minded passion to love and serve Jesus. He alone could comfort her. When He died, she was there. She sought Him even after He was buried. Best of all, He loved and protected her with the same passion with which He loves us all. Reciprocated love is the best kind of love. He loved us first; it is up to us, as Mary did, to reciprocate that love.

Questions: Taken from the reading, complete the following sentences with a short answer.

1. She _____ for Him, as He has for everyone who seeks Him.
2. Weeping, (Mary) would not be _____.
3. Her thoughts were on the _____.
4. She was _____ and not the words of the angels.
5. If one _____ what is in the Gospel story, they will find … a special love.
6. Mary, a person who, in her person, was only _____.
7. Our Lord would not allow any, never even _____, to speak against her.
8. He accused _____ in his own house, for he had an evil thought against her.
9. God's love is for all who _____ and claim to be children of God.

Discussion Questions:

10. We speak in this story of Mary Magdalene. She is a shining example of the love Jesus has for all of us as unique individuals. All we need to do is love Him. We are equals with Mary, a woman once of formerly questionable morals. Knowing that, we dare to accept the love offered to us by God who knows us, knows who we are, and knows what we've done. **What are our best ways to tell others of the love Jesus offers us, and of our love for Him?**

11. If Mary, the sister of Martha, an ordinary sinner, can turn from her past and become a Contemplative, why not us? Jesus loves us for who we are. He loves us, knowing we are already His. Let the most desperate sinner, the Active, the Contemplative, and anyone else seek him. **What verbs would you put in this next sentence? I _____ Him!**

12. This is what matters: the Love of Jesus, our Lord. The last sentence reads, "This is insight into God's love for all who belong and believe and claim to be children of God." To belong, believe, and claim, this is what he asks in return for his love. As with Mary, He loves each of us, first and best. With God, we are all tied for first in being the most beloved. The world tells us to proudly be first alone, not tied. **Share your feelings of being only "tied for first."**

Final Word: It's a love story! It transcends all class, economics, cultures, and social strata. Mary met her redeemer and savior, and she did not merely follow Him, but she gave up all, even sinful ways, to be with Him and learn from Him. May we all feel such passion for Him in our quest for spiritual growth. In your life, may "Jesus" be the answer to all your questions. Amen.

The Cloud of Unknowing   CHAPTER TWENTY-THREE: Enough is All (72-73)

Review: This story is one to be considered over and over, deeper and deeper. John claimed to be "The disciple Jesus loved." It is a title we who seek Him can claim for ourselves. Who are you? You are the disciple Jesus loved. You are. The story of Mary and Jesus is your story.

Today's Reading: Chapter 22 says this, in so many words, "Relax, the Lord defends us." We need not speak against those who speak against us. The Lord will answer for us in spirit, He will meet us with the necessities, and He knows our needs. There is life wisdom in this title, *Enough is All*. It means "be satisfied and trust God."

Questions: Taken from the reading, complete the following sentences with a short answer.

1. We ought to lovingly conform _____ to the Lord Jesus.
2. As needed, He will answer those who _____ against us.
3. We _____ whatever some say or think against us.
4. The Lord will answer _____ in the spirit.
5. We show we will not leave _____ for the worries of the world.
6. _____ will come to those who are Contemplatives.
7. The devil is in their heart and robs them _____.
8. As Mary did, who chose to be meek beneath the _____ of God.
9. For those people who have God … they need _____.

Discussion Questions:

10. As Jesus defended Mary, Lazarus's sister, so does he defend us. Paragraph two says we don't need to defend ourselves, but trust Jesus. This may seem a difficult thing to do as others attack, mock, and criticize us, but we don't need to defend ourselves. We trust God while we go on with the work given us. Enough is all we need. **How can you tell and show the world you are content with God alone?**
11. People living in their own world will attack Contemplatives and Actives for being lazy and self-indulgent, etc. With their limited worldview, they tell us that if we want to work for God, do it after we retire, but now we should be earning for our future. God doesn't ask anything else from us other than we answer that call of God. **Spiritually and physically, where do you want to be?**
12. The chapter ends with the assurance that God will meet our needs adequately. It has worked for others for centuries. At first it may be difficult to believe God is willing and capable of meeting our needs. **How does it help others to see that God meets our needs?**

Final Word: I tell people that God talks to me all the time and says the same thing, over and over: "Shut up and do it." Now, I've never actually heard the voice of God; I've never gotten a divine message telling me to do that, but my life is better when I do it. God might just as well say, "Stop worrying, I can handle it," when I have a problem or need. Enough is all we need; we don't necessarily need more. Trust God.

The Cloud of Unknowing   **CHAPTER TWENTY-FOUR:** Two Loves (74-75)

Review: As this third section comes to an end, we have seen how our lives are lived out in the Martha and Mary story. We are called to love the Lord in all meekness, to trust the Lord in all things, and to do good and honest physical works of mercy and charity. These are the words we need to know and to heed. Contemplative or Active, the Lord needs us all.

Today's Reading: This is a marvelous chapter. Briefly it tells us to put away all charity, desire only God, not to be troubled when you are being troubled, to love God for God's sake alone, and to love everyone and no one. Your family is everyone, none more special. It ends with the thought that we should do as much good as possible. This is revolutionary!

Questions: Taken from the reading, complete the following sentences with a short answer.

1. In the Cloud of Unknowing, all virtues are discarded, especially _____.
2. _____ is nothing but the way to begin and increase your understanding.
3. Life is directed at nothing but for _____.
4. _____ would be fulfilled when love is given.
5. A _____ won't attempt to endure any thought of anything else God made.
6. The _____ of charity where your love for your fellow Christian is.
7. This _____ found will have no special beholding to anyone.
8. _____ you meet is considered to be part of your family.
9. You are led to them to do as much _____.

Discussion Questions:

10. Finally, here is a self-contained definition of Meekness: it is "the blind little love that … can only be fully knowable when one is lost within the Great Cloud of Unknowing." It is what we find when we've put away and forgotten all our virtues, especially charity. It is shocking and it is real. Service for God is enough. Meekness is like a spiritual tattoo on those obedient to God's will. There's no "You" then, only God. **What might motivate you to be so meek?**
11. We have two loves; the greater love is for all that is of God. That should be our everything. Also, there is a lesser love. The world is content with this lesser love, the love of your fellow Christians, a love that has no beholding to anyone, friend or foe, strangers or family. We have lived in this lesser love and called it church, fellowship, social responsibility, but it is not God. **What does it take to move from the Lesser to the Greater of the Loves?**
12. As we leave this third section of this book, reread this chapter. It is short but theologically solid. This is about a calling the world may never recognize. They could well translate it to mean that you were a nice person who loved everyone, maybe a Mother Teresa-type. **How would you describe such a state of service to all?**

Final Word: Does this chapter ask too much of us? Yes. Can we do it? No. But with God's presence, help, and guidance, it happens. Chapter 24 moves us from background to actual work. The future now lies before us. In the following chapters, we will receive our work assignments. Fear not; blunder forth. You will find God awaits us.

Section IV: The Work

The Cloud of Unknowing   CHAPTER TWENTY-FIVE: One Little Act of Love (76-78)

Review: Section IV changes the focus of the book. We have covered what the callings are, how we start, and then given the example of Martha and Mary as role models that can be applied to our own lives. The next five sections answer this little question: How? God knows we are weak, fickle, selfish, and stupid; it is from these raw materials he makes great accomplishments. The preparation is done; let us get on with our real journey.

Today's Reading: This chapter is less concerned with the "little act" as it is with the one who does that act. A little reminder, consider again what we've taken as our goal. We speak of equality. We are not special; those we encounter are not special. By being there, we love them, but we don't attach any special affection toward individuals. We are to be an unbiased testimony of God with our lives, loving equally and serving fairly, without regard to the individual. Then, in the fifth paragraph is the information for which we've been searching.

Questions: Taken from the reading, complete the following sentences with a short answer.

1. You should have no _____ for anyone in this life.
2. Everything else must be _____ which does not add to the love.
3. _____ asks much, especially when directed to a former foe.
4. All are to be loved equally by the _____.
5. As all were _____, yet all people, …, can be saved.
6. The proof that this work does bear [results] is _____.
7. _____ is striving for the salvation of all our brothers and sisters.
8. All who will _____ from God can be saved.
9. Everything in the world _____ God's love.

Discussion Questions:

10. This chapter tells us to have no special attachment to anyone in this life. You are to love your mother, those who hate you, and strangers, all with the same selfless love. It is not hard because it is the right thing to do; they are all family (see p. 75). This is a Contemplative's way. **Discuss whether you think you can ever love them all with the same passion?** (Hint: don't tell your mother that she is loved equally with the worst person in her life.)
11. The work of all who serve God, along with the Actives and Contemplatives, we are all called to strive for the salvation of all our brothers and sisters. Anyone who leaves sin and asks for mercy from God will be saved. This is the virtue paid for by Christ's Passion. This is a mighty work done by meek people, to lead others to Jesus. **Talk about it. How might you participate in this work?**
12. As you speak and they hear your words and see your manner, Christ can use you. Your least act of love, sharing the source of your joy, can bring Salvation to a lost soul. This is not to your credit or glory; this glory belongs to God alone! Will you do it? **Please share your feelings, doubts, stories, and joys caused by God using you.**

Final Word: There is one bridge over death that connects life to Salvation. Be the guide and not the toll taker, the sharer, or the keeper. Do this is one little act of love.

The Cloud of Unknowing   CHAPTER TWENTY-SIX: Salvation for Others (79-80)

Review: The previous chapter should have been called Salvation, except it was less about Salvation than it was of that act of love that brought the hope and the Word to the world. Let all who believe and ask for mercy from God can be saved. If no one tells them, if no one teaches them, how can they learn? This act of love is opening the door and letting them in.

Today's Reading: Chapter 26 tells you to examine your own credentials. Do not ask others to believe in things you do not believe in; do not expect them to seek Salvation unless you, yourself, are certain you are saved. We will lead no one to Salvation, which remains God's work only; yet if we are clean and whole and repentant, God may use us in this work.

Questions: Taken from the reading, complete the following sentences with a short answer.

1. Before you labor for others, start _____ into this high Cloud of Unknowing.
2. Whosoever will pursue this work must _____ in this difficult task.
3. A calling is made, but it is from _____.
4. God seeks the soul _____, usually one who has doing it.
5. Only done with the help of the grace of God, this is _____.
6. What may have seemed impossible, soon it will seem only a _____.
7. God works _____, and God works when the time is right.
8. That work belongs to God only and without God _____.
9. It is better to _____ than to ignore it.

Discussion Questions:

10. In the second paragraph of today's reading, we are told to seek salvation for others. This is a high calling and a work that not all are called for. It may be the hardest task we could be called to do, or the very best. Have you ever been in a situation when you were asked to explain salvation? If you are in a group, this might be a good exercise to explain what is meant by salvation. If you are alone, write it down. **Explain salvation as the monk uses the term in this book.**
11. We cannot move alone, for God will always be with us. Sometimes we say words that change another's life. Assume it was God using our words and us, but it is not we ourselves who do anything. God is always ready to help and seeks for the soul who is ready to share the Gospel. Have you had an incident where you said something or heard something that changed a life? **If you have experienced this, tell what happened and what your emotional reaction was afterward.**
12. When we were missionaries, it felt as if we were under the umbrella of God's presence. When we retired, I feared we'd move from that shelter, but in truth the umbrella is still there. We still rely on it. God protects faithful servants with a presence in our lives. **Share any stories or insights you have regarding God's presence protecting you in your life.**

Final Word: To be the person who God uses to help another find the path that leads to the Clouds of Darkness and Unknowing is to know that this is not your work, but God's. To be the agent the first time seems impossible; by the tenth time it will seem natural. Be brave, be bold, and be willing. Salvation is a gift beyond description; share it with others.

The Cloud of Unknowing   CHAPTER TWENTY-SEVEN: Who Will Labor? (81)

Review: Leading others to Salvation is not the only work of Christians, but it's probably the most important. If you are one with that grace, share it freely.

Today's Reading: Chapter 27 is one paragraph long and contains 108 words. It will not have nine questions or three discussion questions. It does, however, give assignments to those who choose to be Contemplatives rather than those who choose the Martha role of Actives. Contemplatives are to seek out those desiring Salvation. Also, noted again, when you seek God earnestly, your past sins will not burden you.

Questions: Taken from the reading, complete the following sentences with a short answer.

1. First and foremost, those who labor for the salvation of others in this work must:

   know _____,

   2. by _____,

   3. and with _____.

4. The answer to whom should do this work is _____,

   5. and those who _____,

   6. but _____.

7. This applies to all who _____,

   8. no matter who they are, whether _____.

Discussion Question:

9. Who among you is willing to work for the salvation of others? Your answer is:

   The one who _____

   _____

   _____

Final Word: Our monk friend is not yet done trying to recruit us to take positions with which we are not comfortable. We need people like this in our lives, ones who are not afraid to ask us difficult questions or encourage us to take on difficult tasks. It seems that many who are willing remain unable and many who are able are unwilling. This particular request, launched six and a half centuries ago, was aimed at you in the here and now. Our monk was the arrow, but God was the bowman.

The Cloud of Unknowing **CHAPTER TWENTY-EIGHT:** The Work of Salvation (82-83)

Review: Did that last chapter make your heart quake? If it did, this is a good book for you. Your answer did not have to be, "Yeah, Lord. Send me!" But some who read that chapter will say, "It is I you seek!" and go into a new phase of ministry. Others will say, "No, not I!" But most will wonder, "Really, is it I?" If it is, God will recruit you; if it is not you, God will send other work for you. Be at peace.

Today's Reading: Sometimes we wait to see what purpose God will call us, knowing it will be a harder work than we've ever known. It's up to us to prepare ourselves. For that work, let us turn to Chapter 28 and read. Do not think of this as preparing yourself for the labors of Salvation only, but for any work done for God and the Kingdom of God.

Questions: Taken from the reading, complete the following sentences with a short answer.

1. They should not begin to labor until they have _____.
2. Souls must dry up both the _____.
3. _____ alone will not accomplish this task, no matter how sincere.
4. Even if one has never sinned in deed, _____.
5. The pain of the Original Sin will forever _____.
6. Sin will keep itself between _____ of this pain.
7. This Cloud is a _____ done by God.
8. We have allowed ourselves to be willfully _____.
9. _____ lost the place it ought to have possessed.

Discussion Questions:

10. Those who seek to do the work of leading others to Salvation generally need to have cleansed their conscience according to their faith and to have lived a life that is unsoiled by sin and reputation. That's a good start and a daunting standard. No one is ever ready to do this work, they just begin and trust God to make it possible or not. **How would you begin?**
11. The pain of Original Sin is real. It is an obstruction between God and us. Examine your life; do you see evidence of that sin in your life? Being human, we must live with that legacy. It's difficult to explain Original Sin and its consequences if you don't know yourself. **Explain this Original Sin in non-theological words, perhaps as you would to a ten-year-old.**
12. The Cloud of Unknowing is described as "a righteous act done by God." **Share your opinion; does the Cloud protect God from us or are we protected from God's presence?**

Final Word: A bad analogy: think of finding Salvation like washing dishes. Some pots and pans need scrubbing, others have a coating that is Teflon©-like and the gunk falls away. The merits of the pot can't be seen until it's clean. Sometimes the cleansing is a long, backbreaking effort; other times the dirt falls away. Clean your own pots first. The last clause in the second paragraph is "Cleansing is in order."

The Cloud of Unknowing   CHAPTER TWENTY-NINE: Who Is Saved? (84-85)

Review: The unavoidable problem is sin. Period. Being human, the ability to sin comes naturally. We will forever be human, but the goal is not to allowing ourselves to accept the easy path or our sinful nature. The struggle is to recognize that sin is within us and then resist it. Do what is right even though the best we can do isn't good enough. At some point, we will surrender to God and trust our cleansing to God. God can do what we can't.

Today's Reading: The key to today's reading can be found in the third paragraph: "Expect the Day of Judgment to be wonderful." We've been reading about sin and of the weighty burden of evil from which there seems no escape. What is the answer? Judgment! On that day you will see yourself as God sees you. Some who are convinced they are vile will see they are clean; others, assuming they have done better than those around them, will find themselves overburdened with the sins they denied. It is miraculous; it is our hope.

Questions: Taken from the reading, complete the following sentences with a short answer.

1. Who can be saved? Anyone _____.
2. Seeking to win back that innocence that was lost, expect to _____.
3. By _____ those who have been greater sinners must labor.
4. The most horrible and habitual sinners have come to _____.
5. This is the _____ of our Lord Jesus who grants them grace.
6. For this reason, expect the _____ to be wonderful.
7. _____ will be the ones to sit rightfully with the saints.
8. Some who seemed holy will sit in full sorrow among _____.
9. _____ any one in this life, not even considering good or evil.

Discussion Questions:

10. Who will be saved is best answered by the sentence, "I don't know" (Chapter 6, p. 31). However, sometimes it is difficult to resist opinions on that or any judgment. Have you ever had a secret opinion only to realize you were absolutely wrong in your assumption? **Please share any such incident for, truly, we've all done it.**
11. Some people anticipate the Day of Judgment as the day when they will be proven right; others fear that Day for the opposite reason. On that day there will be Grace and the Cross. There will be guilt when nothing can be denied. All will be revealed. **What brings you comfort and peace in facing such a wonderful and dreadful Day of Judgment?**
12. Good people can do evil and evil people can do good. The final judgment will not be based on our human standards but on God's infinite insight and wisdom. It is best if we don't judge, yet sometimes discernment is both wise and necessary. There is a difference between Christian discernment and legal judgment. **Please share your opinions on the differences.**

Final Word: We will never judge ourselves. We know ourselves only through our biased eyes and desires. I think everyone who goes through judgment will be amazed at the final verdict; all will try to tell the judge that the judgment was wrong. The sinful will deny their sinfulness as strongly as the sainted will deny their goodness. We are judged on what we do, say, think, and feel. I don't know who I am.

The Cloud of Unknowing   CHAPTER THIRTY: Judges (86)

Review: Who is saved? Born under the burden of sin, living in a vile world, our passions fired by evil intentions, none are worthy of Salvation. God will not lower the standards by which we are judged, rather God sent Jesus, "So that everyone who believes in him will not perish but have eternal life" (John 3:16, NRSV). It's not what we do; it's what Jesus did. It's a matter of faith.

Today's Reading: God appointed judges. Male and female, God appointed them. Some were terrible (Samson) and some were good (Gideon). Any human judge will fail; none are perfect. Those who follow the Law do what a judge should do; those who show mercy do what the Lord would do; and those who can be bought and are biased will be judged accordingly. None but those who God calls should be judges. That includes us.

Questions: Taken from the reading, complete the following sentences with a short answer.

1. Judges in this world are _____ fellow creatures.
2. Judges are only those ... over their fellow creatures _____.
3. They judge on _____ that are given by the statutes of the laws.
4. Judges "be aware that they _____ to take upon themselves the judgment."
5. They who dare to judge will _____ in their judgments.
6. Even as you act as judge of yourself, this is a matter between _____.
7. Between you and your God or between you and your _____.

Discussion Questions:

8. Human judges rule on the basis of the evidence; divine judgment is based on truths that are not necessarily the facts. Human law has little mercy; in divine matters Grace usually prevails. **Explore the difference between evidence, truth, facts, and mercy.**
9. Human judges err. The innocent have been convicted under the rules of law. Divine Judgment will be the truth mingled with Grace. Before you stand before Divine Judgment, it is important that you know yourself. Do not find out then that you are a stranger to yourself. **Discuss how difficult it is for anyone to ever know his or her "real self?"**
10. When you serve on a jury, they demand that you form your judgments on facts, not on opinions. Discernment is easiest when it is based on facts, but there's a gut-feeling inclination, both positive and negative, to form you own opinion. That's not what they want. **If you have any good jury stories of passing judgment, please share them.**

Final Word: My illustration of Divine Judgment is that Satan opens up the books of the charges against us and finds only blank pages, for God's Grace has cleansed us in all ways. Satan screams, "It's not fair!" Satan is right, it isn't fair: it's Grace. Grace outperforms the Law. Grace is not justice; it is Grace. Grace is God's final proof that only God is God. Human judges can show mercy but Grace is from God alone.

The Cloud of Unknowing   CHAPTER THIRTY-ONE: Burying your Thoughts (87-88)

Review: God appointed judges and some were good: Samuel, Othniel, Ehud, and Deborah. Some judges were not so good: Samson. My wife thinks Gideon was the best and worst judge, in the beginning he was good, but in the end he raised a false idol, an ephod, in the land. Judges judge, that's what they do. We are blessed because we get the Lord as our judge.

Today's Reading: This is a good news/bad news chapter. As we move away from all that judgment, in Chapter 31 we will speak of the trials we endure. This is a preparation for the judgment and what we can do to prepare ourselves.

Questions: Taken from the reading, complete the following sentences with a short answer.

1. A time will come when you feel you _____ to amend yourself.
2. This will mark the beginning of the time when _____.
3. You need to forever be _____ to step away from these thoughts.
4. You must endeavor to cover those _____ with the thickness of the Cloud.
5. You must _____ as soon as they occur.
6. You must put them (thoughts) down _____ as often as they arise.
7. If you think the trial is _____, you may seek other methods.
8. _____ can reveal to you which methods are best.
9. God has _____ than you will find in anyone in this life.

Discussion Questions:

10. Carrying on from the previous chapter, this chapter begins by asking you if you've made amends that satisfy the standards and expectations of your church. **With your church in mind, what would be your next step in making personal amends to meet their expectations for you?**
11. One of the unpleasant surprises about self-awareness and amends is that as soon as you correct one fault, another pops up, and then another, and another. You must not stop to savor any apparent victory, but put them behind you quickly, bury them deep in the Cloud of Forgetting. It is not pleasant to realize how deep and numerous our spiritual flaws are. We were born this way. **What struggle did you think you'd be able to overcome but have not?**
12. If you have followed these directives, you will come to the place where the only source of wisdom you have is to turn to God. When we find there's no one but God, we are in a good place. God's way is a path of wisdom. **Share an experience where you turned to God for wisdom**

Final Word: Strangely, when we have worked hard to make amends regarding our shortcomings, no one ever says, "I am done." Those who seek to know themselves know that it is impossible. Generally, those who claim to be perfectionists only dare to approach the pettiest things to control. But a moment comes when we realize the enormity of the task, which is when we will sigh in complete dismay and turn our cares over to God and to God alone. God will not make us perfect in this world, but we will be cleared to proceed.

The Cloud of Unknowing   CHAPTER THIRTY-TWO: Cowering (89-90)

Review: What a great place for this chapter! In Chapter 31 we examined ourselves, seeking flaws and making amends, until we realize we cannot go deep enough into our sinful nature to claim any privilege from God. The book said we are to turn to God, but how? Read on!

Today's Reading: Chapter 32 deals with the art of surrendering. This is not a skill anyone teaches; human vanity declares itself unwilling to cower or surrender. I believe the phrase goes, "I'd rather die than surrender!" Oh, how shallow is our vanity. Surrendering is a bold expression of our willingness to change, to accept the authority of another, and to proceed with life. Come, let us learn about cowering and surrendering, lessons we need to endure.

Questions: Taken from the reading, complete the following sentences with a short answer.
1. Dump _____, for they come between you and your God.
2. Try to simply _____, seeking to fix your mind on things that matter.
3. Easily and truly conceived, for it is nothing but admitting the _____.
4. To see God, this desire is _____; it rightfully brings peace.
5. Rather than battle them [your thoughts], you should _____ before them.
6. Through this cowering you _____ to God's mercy.
7. Do this especially if that enemy is _____.
8. Truthful knowing and feeling of yourself as you are, _____.
9. God will also take you up and _____.

Discussion Questions:

10. Heroes don't cower! Exclamation mark! But we aren't heroes; we're wretched sinners who are right to cower. Imagine standing before God and visualize "cowering." This isn't a political gesture: this is awe! **Describe how you might express this divine sense of awe.**

11. It is not folly to be unable to overcome your thoughts of self-glorification, be they dreams of humility or of success in battle. In truth, we'd rather refuse the fight and bury our heads. We do not lie in admitting this. It is too easy to deceive ourselves. **Talk about how difficult and painful it is to face the truth when lies are so much sweeter.**

12. We are human and sinful wretches who, according to the monk, are worse than nothing. Yet, with and through God's awesome glory we can become honorable and faithful servants of our God. Then, against Satan we can stand and fight, but it is before God we should cower. The Bible has many stories of those who fell unconscious before God or his messengers, cowering before them. Consider Daniel, Ezekiel, and the John of Revelation as examples. **How would you describe the kind of awe these characters in the story must have felt?**

Final Word: This chapter reinforces our weak and sinful nature that becomes evident when exposed to things divine. We dare not be bold before God; we cannot hide our sinfulness. When exposed to things divine, it is time to surrender our vain ways. To cower is not necessarily to be afraid; it can be a way to honor God. The fear of the LORD is the beginning of wisdom (Proverbs 9:10, KJV).

The Cloud of Unknowing CHAPTER THIRTY-THREE: The Burden of Original Sin (91-92)

Review: Why are we calling ourselves wretched, sinful, and cowardly? No one else in the world thinks of themselves in those terms. True, but the world does not seek God, does not want to serve anyone but itself, and abounds in concepts such as vanity, deceit, anger, jealousy, and lust. They think they can live without fear of judgment; we know better.

Today's Reading: Chapter 33 is a bit of a mid-term graduation. Loosely speaking, the chapter says you have been a student for the first ninety pages; now is time for you to learn how to be a teacher of others. As we conclude this third section of the book, we are moving into a much-needed "Meditation" section. The original author has set up a curriculum in his book; he concluding with encouraging words that we are on the right path to God.

Questions: Taken from the reading, complete the following sentences with a short answer.

1. Original Sin will be with us always, this is known as the _____.
2. You have the _____ to have tried the proof of these techniques.
3. _____ is a [higher] form of learning.
4. Learn and labor . . . Suffer meekly in the _____.
5. Your flaws can become your own _____.
6. You can be cleansed of both sin and the _____.
7. As for the _____, it will be with you always.
8. A day will come when you will never go back, nor ever again _____.
9. New sins will _____ but they will do little harm.

Discussion Questions:

10. This chapter is titled "The Burden of Original Sin." You can do many things to cleanse yourself of your weaknesses, sins, and flaws, but you can never cleanse yourself of the stain of Original Sin. It is the original birth defect. God can forgive all your sins, but you will still bear the impact of Original Sin until the day you die. **What are some of the ways that help you cope with this burden of sin?**
11. And then, one day, it will happen that your failings no longer burden you. You will accept your flaws as things that don't matter and you will feel secure with the pain of Original Sin. **Assuming you're not yet at this stage, imagine how it might feel if your sins were mere inconveniences and not an overpowering burden.**
12. In that day, new sins and desires will still fall on you but be unable to land, finding it impossible to stick to you. Then you will examine yourself again and wonder what the problem had been. The wisely named Cloud of Forgetting is a gift from God. Are you ready for that new state? **Try to describe what it might feel like if you could leave your old sins behind like a broken habit.**

Final Word: It is the purpose of this book to enlighten you in various ways and to give your life a direction and destination. It is very presumptive of the author to assume we wanted or needed to change, yet he gives us the means to change. Believe this is actually the work of God using an anonymous monk centuries ago to bring this message to us. Let the message of this book change you and bring you closer to God.

Section V: Meditation

The Cloud of Unknowing   CHAPTER THIRTY-FOUR: One Way (93-95)

Review: This new section called "Meditation" takes our focus from the sins of the world and our flaws and brings us to a new place: the inner self. Each of us is different and we are all the same; sinners we are and servants of God we will be, each called of us to a different role.

Today's Reading: This chapter has more data than usual, hence we will have 16 short answer questions taken from the text and only two discussion questions. The focus has clearly changed. This is not a section on how to meditate; this explains why we should.

Questions: Taken from the reading, complete the following sentences with a short answer.

1. You are able to come to this work of being a _____.
2. Being a Contemplative [comes] only through _____.
3. Open for those chosen souls, chosen without _____.
4. Christ chooses _____ than those who have never grieved Him.
5. God actually calls sinners, _____.
6. In this, God is seen as being _____.
7. There is no soul _____, nor one unable to receive this.
8. Grace is given not only to _____, nor is it withheld because of sin.
9. Beware of pride, for it is _____ of God.
10. Meekness: no soul has the ability to become a Contemplative _____.
11. Be at peace, for you never need _____.
12. Be _____; do look upon your life to judge yourself.
13. Steer away from the _____, for the desire to know will hinder you.
14. I urge you to trust fully _____ will and desires.
15. It may be done by this devil who is _____.
16. All good things depend upon _____ and there is no other means.

Discussion Questions:

17. It certainly seems God loves sinners and chooses them to do the work that needs to be done in the world. There may be nothing in the world God loves more than a repentant sinner. **Assuming this to be true, what words would you use to tell a friend about this extraordinary grace of God?**
18. The author mentions the devil again; in other places he calls him Satan, deceiver, etc. These are relevant issues, becoming more important as we progress through this book and through life. **Discuss what you believe evil is and what the devil's role in the world is.**

Final Word: This chapter is magnificent. It leaves me panting for air and drives me to reread it over and again. In my margin I've written: "This grace or disgrace?" I pray we choose "This grace."

The Cloud of Unknowing CHAPTER THIRTY-FIVE: Lessons, Meditations, & Prayer (96-97)

Review: Have you caught your breath after that last chapter? In this Fifth Section, the book has increased in its intensity. God's Grace was woven throughout those three pages. May you later come back to this book and read only that one chapter. If you are still reading, you are on your way to becoming a Contemplative. Congratulations.

Today's Reading: This is a chapter you should carry in your heart as you go through the days ahead; it is the map that shows you the way you should precede. The last line in the chapter is priceless advice.

Questions: Taken from the reading, complete the following sentences with a short answer.

1. Grace is the only way to _____.
2. Be occupied especially in those things involving your _____, _____ & _____.
3. Given to those walking along on that path to perfection, but it is _____.
4. _____ may not be a good thing without the reading and hearing.
5. God's work, whether written or spoken, is like _____.
6. Spiritually, this mirror can be like _____.
7. Without reading or hearing God's Word, … a soul [is] _____.
8. _____ can be good if it stands alone in the dark.
9. There can be no prayer that occurs without _____.

Discussion Questions:

10. There are countless people (God knows the actual number) who believe their good works and life style will save them. This book says, "Grace is the only way to Salvation." Jesus says, "I am the Way." **Be still and meditate on this statement, writing down your thoughts, sharing them with others.**
11. If I didn't have mirrors in my house, I'd never know how old I'd become. The mirror shows me things I don't always want to know. It shows me the truth. Likewise, God's word, spoken or written, should be examined like the image in the mirror. In the Bible we see the truth, whether we like it or not. God is not afraid of revealing the truth; the question is, are we ready and willing to deal with it? **God's Word is a Mirror. What truth do you wish to avoid seeing?**
12. It doesn't exactly say this, but Christian community helps keep us on the right path. Taking our own path, finding our own interpretations, seeking alien knowledge, or keeping our thoughts secret can cause us to lose our way. A mediocre church is better than no church; Christian fellowship doesn't necessarily involve a church building; and a good pastor / teacher / leader can be a trustworthy guide. **Why should you read, study, and pray while thinking and meditating on these subjects?**

Final Word: Use your brain. Tread boldly and cautiously. Trust not yourself, trust others less, and trust God fully to guide and protect you. God can use some strange means to keep us where we ought to be. Trust God; all else will follow.

The Cloud of Unknowing   CHAPTER THIRTY-SIX: Words (98-99)

Review: Grace is the only way to Salvation along a path that is open to all. Our logic and opinions and wishes are dead-ends. Grace and Bible readings, meditations, and prayer are the luggage we want to carry with us. God's Word is the mirror that is the only way we can ever truly see ourselves without our lying vanity deceiving us. Some vanity tries to make us look better; some vanities try to make us look worse, unlovable, ugly, and unworthy.

Today's Reading: This chapter is a deepening of what we covered in Chapter 5. Here, in the first paragraph, we read that we cannot pray meaningfully without thinking. This is not freethinking; this is pondering our own wretchedness and the goodness of God. Between these extremes, we find deep words on which to focus, often beyond our understanding.

Questions: Taken from the reading, complete the following sentences with a short answer.

1. _____ may well have been lessons from God and not learned.
2. Have no meditations other than those on _____.
3. Do not be overly profound in your _____.
4. Do not expound upon these words ... lest you _____.
5. Find special words and hold them as _____.
6. Hold _____ as if it were a lump that you never will understand.
7. Knowing this lump is nothing other _____.
8. Be without _____ whether you are sitting or going.
9. There can be no _____ without _____.

Discussion Questions:

10. The first paragraph ends: "There are some things earthly teachers cannot teach you." Then he explains how we are expected to learn these "things." **By what criteria do we judge these insights and blind feelings? Are they are of God or are they creatures of our own vanity and self-delusion?**
11. Some prayers are answered before they are prayed, some questions are answered before asked, and some individuals receive a "sudden insight and blind feeling" without reason. **If you know or have heard of any such experiences, or if there are any examples of this you might have experienced, please share them.**
12. In the middle of the second paragraph are the words: "Do not be overly profound in your definitions." We can define a word, an idea, or a friendship to death, and we end up with nothing. If we think we can fully understand the deeper things, then often this indicates we have too shallow of an understanding of it. **Please restate what the phrase "overly profound" means to you.**

Final Word: Sometimes you have to quit thinking and just accept the words. This does not mean to stop thinking, but merely do not overthink what you read and how you define words or directions. A profoundly simple faith is a source of great strength. You do not have to define every word; sometimes you can just treasure it.

The Cloud of Unknowing   CHAPTER THIRTY-SEVEN: One Word (100-1)

Review: Chapter 36 was about finding our way. It told us to think as we prayed and not to reject our insights and feelings without examining them. By meditating on our state, we will grow. God is to be our focus. Treat sin as if it were something foul; examine our word. Learn to be without "fluctuation of countenance," meaning: Let us be consistent in our manner.

Today's Reading: There is power in even a single word—both positively and negatively. A single word can motivate you, it can deceive you, it can help maintain your vows and life or it can betray all you stand for. One word is precious; watch even your smallest words.

Questions: Taken from the reading, complete the following sentences with a short answer.

1. As we labor, never forget that _____ which enables us to work.
2. Pray as we have been taught, but special prayers rise suddenly _____.
3. If your prayers are offered in words, then it is best if you _____.
4. Truly, _____ the better.
5. A single _____ is better than a word of two syllables.
6. They burst out loudly with a great spirit, and they cry but _____.
7. It evokes a response. So, too, does _____.
8. [A little word] is _____ driven from the depth of the spirit.
9. A short prayer _____ most quickly.

Discussion Questions:

10. This would be a good time to reread Chapter 7, pp. 33-35. This is a subject we will return to later in the book, but the writer wants us to find a good, one-syllable word that we find holy, a word that harmonizes with ourselves. Make it your private mantra. Its design is to keep distracting thoughts from stealing your focus." Since reading Chapter 7, have you found much distraction when you try to speak your word? **What was the most common source of your distractions?**
11. The next to the last sentence in Chapter 37 boldly states, "a single, small word pierces the ear of Almighty God more than does long Psalter, unmindfully mumbled in the mouth." But, what our good monk does not say is that a Psalm, read slowly and with meaning, in a heart-felt manner, pierces the heart of the one who prays it. Take a psalm (1, 25, 27, 32, 63, 91, and/or 103 as examples) and read it aloud to God as if your very Salvation depended on your reading. It doesn't, but meaningful prayer is priceless treasure. **What was it like for you when you prayerfully and spiritually read a psalm?**
12. Imagine you're driving on an icy road and the car begins to lose traction as an avalanche descends on you, try this one word prayer, "God!" **It is adequate, isn't it? Please discuss.**

Final Word: I love this chapter in that it reveals that words have power and effect. Most words I speak are spoken and never considered again. Words said in prayer are like tattoos; they stay with you. Seriously, do read a Psalm prayerfully; you'll love it. A one-word prayer is good, so is a long prayer, and anything between.

The Cloud of Unknowing **CHAPTER THIRTY-EIGHT:** Height, Depth, Breadth, Length

Review: To pray is like ringing the doorbell on the house of God. God will hear the smallest click or the longest ring. But the short prayer is often preferred because it focuses your mind and heart on one sound, one aspect. It becomes your sound; it is one of your connections to God. Your word is a precious treasure, a gem. Guard it lovingly and boldly.

Today's Reading: Chapter 38 is a legalist's paradise. It tries to speak of the dimensions of God in regard to length, breadth, height, and depth. I would have said God's way is a little longer than infinity and a little wider than forever. This is not the monk's best chapter, but we'll still learn something about God in it.

Questions: Taken from the reading, complete the following sentences with a short answer.

1. Short prayers, in full spirit, offers the _____, _____, _____, & _____.
2. Long sentences get _____.
3. A little syllable can better contain the _____.
4. It is something only a soul can comprehend, _____ for heaven.
5. Not fully but in a partial manner, we pray in _____.
6. Everlastingness of God is _____; God's love is _____;
   God's might is _____, and God's wisdom is _____.
7. Within you is a kinship resulting from _____.
8. A compassionate soul is made to be merciful _____.
9. Mercifulness and kindness are things that are had by _____.

Discussion Questions:

10. The monk who wrote this book lived in the Lake District of England in the late 1300s. I imagine he would find it difficult to adapt to our media-rich world. Even in those slow-moving times he wanted to avoid getting "bogged down" by too much verbiage. He wanted "a little syllable to contain the weight of our spirit." One way to look at his advice is to be encouraged to speak less and listen more. **How do we train ourselves to speak less and listen more? Perhaps even more difficult, how can we encourage those around us to do likewise?**
11. The fourth paragraph focuses on your enemy needing your help. **Tell why you would or wouldn't help a proven enemy who was found needing help.**
12. Much of this section of the book (chapters 34-42) encourages a simplification and an inner directing of our lives. It isn't easy to simplify. **What could you do to simplify your life?**

Final Word: The writer wants us to take some scale of the "size" of God to prove our own insignificance. Our measure comes from mercy and kindness, qualities given to us by God although we can do nothing to deserve this Grace. When we are blessed by God, our insignificance is a power to be reckoned with. We are shown this: keep it simple.

The Cloud of Unknowing   CHAPTER THIRTY-NINE: The Single Word (104-5)

Review: These are my words, not the monk's: Imagine ourselves as atoms comparing ourselves to the universe. Yet, through the Grace of God, we are blessed by the gift of mercy, forgiveness, and kindness. The monk's version is to keep our prayers in relative size as compared to God's standards. He felt the immensity of God.

Today's Reading: We are once again told to keep our prayers simple, a single word, one-syllable. And though the prayer itself is short, by praying often you keep your mind, heart, and soul on God and away from your own concerns. Take your simple word and allow God to stir that word within you.

Questions: Taken from the reading, complete the following sentences with a short answer.

1. When you pray, you do not need to use _____.
2. The word of your choosing must be _____.
3. It is true that all evil can be _____.
4. Do not dwell on the meaning of your sins, but _____.
5. If you intently pray, … say no more than this single word, "_____."
6. All that is good and all that is evil as these _____ cover.
7. But do not study, _____, for by doing so you'll never come to the purpose.
8. _____ are never acquired by study, but only by grace.
9. Take those words for yourself as _____.

Discussion Questions:

10. In keeping it simple, the two words, SIN and GOD, are probably the key building blocks of our spiritual walk. Simple but heavy and focused, these words are the depth, height, length, and breadth of the spirit. Can you keep your prayer life so simple? **What happens in your mind when you meditate using only these two special words?**
11. The words "Help" or "Fire" evoked reactions instantly. Today we could shout the heart-stopping word, "Shooter," and get strangers running. Would you want to react so emotionally to the word SIN that you burned with shame, or so emotionally awed with the word GOD? Try to imagine yourself with that kind of focus as our monk sought. **What internal reaction do you have for these two words: SIN and GOD?**
12. The world seems to conspire against us when we try to simplify life. A third word, short and with three-letters and one-syllable that we painfully hear is this one: BUT. Most of our faith statements and desires end with "but" and not with "Amen." "I'd love to, but—," "We would, but—," "I'd have done it, but—." Do not let BUT be your holy word. **Share some of those "BUT" moments that caused you pain, joy, or frustration.**

Final Word: "Keeping it simple" are words from the fourth paragraph. It is complicated to live simply. It is a difficult idea to apply such a philosophy to our lives. An odd creature, I once lived in a ten-by-ten foot shack in the Cascade Mountains for twelve years. In many ways, they were the best years of my life. BUT I can't go back. Sadly, I'll forever miss that simplicity.

The Cloud of Unknowing   CHAPTER FORTY: Both Words (106-8)

Review: Chapter 39 emphasized two very different words: SIN and GOD. They represent the spectrum of our life, from one extreme to the opposite. We live our lives on that vast plain between those words. They define us. Yet they are the two walls between which we must live and strive.

Today's Reading: Neither of those two words, GOD and SIN, is deniable. Both have a purpose in our lives as we carry them in our hearts and souls. This chapter will explain why we don't want to reject one and carry the other only.

Questions: Taken from the reading, complete the following sentences with a short answer.

1. Fill your spirit with the _____.
2. Contemplatives think all sin is _____.
3. Contemplatives consider each sin as being _____.
4. The real substance of sin is, most often, nothing _____.
5. Fill your spirit with the spiritual meaning of _____.
6. There is _____ that will be worked in one's soul without God's grace.
7. God is everything, both _____.
8. There should be nothing in either your mind or your will but _____.
9. If you have ___, then you should lack ___; if you lack ___, you should have ___.

Discussion Questions:

10. When we pray about SIN, our focus needs to be on ourselves. It is not that we need to recall every sin, but that we are to be ever aware of our unworthiness as we dare to seek God. We don't have to tell God about our sins; we can be certain that God knows about them already. Likewise, when we pray to GOD, we don't try to understand, define, or evaluate the things of God. To meditate on God and acknowledge God is everything; it is all we need think about. We need not pray and tell God what to do. **For what should the saints pray every day?**

11. An easier discussion subject: It says we "will always feel, in some way, the burden of this foul, stinking lump of sin. It is as if it were united and congealed with the very substance of your own being." It's a terrible description of us according to our monk-friend. We should hate our own sin and yet, with full assurance, know that God loves us the way we are. **As best you can, please share your feelings about this amazing paradox.**

12. Set a timer for three minutes, then remain silent and try to focus only on these two words: SIN and GOD. Time will probably feel long during those three minutes and short afterwards. This may seem like three minutes of examining yourself in a mirror. **Try it and then share your feelings during that time of silent contemplation, as you are comfortable.**

Final Word: Do not fill your spirit with SIN, but only the "spiritual meaning of the word." Fill your spirit with GOD and experience Grace and Forgiveness, but do not worry about defining it. Make this a resting point on our journey through the book.

The Cloud of Unknowing   CHAPTER FORTY-ONE In Sickness and in Health (109-110)

Review: Chapter 40 was almost an unexpected final exam in this fifth section called "Meditations." The two words are the boulders in our backpacks we've been carrying up this long hill. Their purpose was to make us stronger. This last chapter brought us to the top of the hill. The next two chapters are easier; the ground is more level. Hope abounds.

Today's Reading: If we are on a true spiritual journey, shouldn't life get easier? No, there will be illnesses and doubts because, sometimes, the easiest places turn out to be the most difficult. Chapter 41 warns us and encourages us, the sort of thing we'd hope a friend would do. There is encouragement in this chapter.

Questions: Taken from the reading, complete the following sentences with a short answer.

1. What sorts of discretion do we need in order to become a Contemplative? _____!
2. In the things you do, you should have _____ in eating, drinking, sleeping, etc.
3. Remain discreet so they will never become too _____.
4. These _____ will try to drag you down from the intended spiritual heights.
5. In earnestness or in folly, meaning, you will have them _____.
6. You ought never to be the cause of your own _____.
7. Let _____ in your body and soul, keeping you in good health.
8. If sickness does come to you, _____.
9. Show yourself to be _____ in times of your trials.

Discussion Questions:

10. God does not take us out of this world, but when we die God welcomes us. God does not cause cancers or illness or birth defects, but God will be there with us. Yet some healings are miraculous. **From your life, share some illness, healings, or death stories that caused you to move either closer to or further from God.**
11. In this life, we ought to pray for good health as much as bad health, for discretion as much as patience. Prayer is a key to our health, service, and peace. Do you pray thankfully for your job, neighbors, garbage collection, rains, *et al.*? Do you thank God for those others in your life? I'd never pray for yard-work, yet I pray for the ability to mow, rake, etc. **For what do you pray that people don't normally pray?**
12. The next to the last sentence reads tells us this: "Show yourself to be faithful in times of your trials." This is our Christian witness to the world. This is a personal witness of our love of God, our family, our friends, and those around us. But there are many we do not know who observe our behavior. Let us be discreet in our pain, suffering, and witness. This doesn't mean you have to be silent. **How might even a prayer of complaint be a witness?**

Final Word: My translation is out, published, in print, and revealing. One of the things it reveals is the difference between discrete and discreet. The second one means to be polite and unmentioned, the first one means to be separated. Confession: I confused them in this chapter, using them apparently at random, and am unable, at this time, to re-edit it. Forgive me. This is a writer's nightmare, again proving my imperfection. Please, be discreet, but be free to discretely laugh at me.

The Cloud of Unknowing   CHAPTER FORTY-TWO: Self-Control (111-112)

Review: "You ought never to cause your own feebleness." I suppose this discreetly includes my spelling. Living in this world demands much perseverance from us to live wholesomely and with a clean disposition. We must continue to learn, working toward a higher standard than the world demands, and keeping our hearts focused on the love God has for us.

Today's Reading: The concluding chapter on "Meditations" is "Self-Control." Self-control is one of the results of deep and faithful meditation. It is not the goal; it is the result. This chapter is a gift you can give to yourself: self-control.

Questions: Taken from the reading, complete the following sentences with a short answer.

1. Wisdom: Take only that which you can _____.
2. Do this without ceasing from your work and without _____.
3. Do this and you will come _____ consideration.
4. Even those people who limit themselves will always _____.
5. You need to experience _____ this spiritual work in your soul.
6. You must crush any _____ in all [ways].
7. You should never be the cause _____.
8. But let the proof of these things be _____.
9. It is _____ you should have, and _____ you should lack.

Discussion Questions:

10. Possess less, desire less, be satisfied, and keep your life simple. Those are good and powerful steps. Unfortunately, these are like the steps Peter took when he stepped out of the boat. The first step seemed to work fine, but then he began to sink until Jesus grabbed him. As we begin to incorporate those steps into our lives, life gets better. If you fail, scripture reminds us that Jesus was there for Peter and is there for us. **Take a few minutes and talk about this Bible story** (Matt. 14:25-32).
11. Question #5 above is from the line, "You need to experience an awakening to fully understand this spiritual work within your soul." But not all people experience this kind of awakening. If you haven't, proceed in your walk; if you have and you are willing, share your experience. **Discuss this sentence from the monk. Why do you agree or disagree with him?**
12. Sinners are sinners; sinners are who they are; and sinners are who we are. It is God we earnestly seek. As we finish this Fifth Section, stop and spiritually examine yourself. If you seek perfection, you are bound to fail; if you seek growth and an increase in understanding, we can rejoice. God is with us; be at peace. **Take a few moments and consider if you are spiritually growing toward the person you wish to be. What evidence is there of this growth?**

Final Word: I have always lived a simple life; always I could have done better. I never desired much, I am easily satisfied, and yet there lurks within me a hunger that I would love to deny, if I could. I feel like a sanctimonious someone secure in the boat telling Peter to step out onto the waters like Jesus was, for God is with us. We are all so wonderfully flawed, I can understand why God would love us. It is true: we are loved. Our existence is proof of that.

Section VI: Lessening the Self

The Cloud of Unknowing   CHAPTER FORTY-THREE: Forgetting Yourself (113-4)

Review: It is GOD we must focus on; it is SIN we must wrestle with to prepare ourselves for what comes next. The goodness of God will help us, for now is the time when we have need for this witnessing word! Amen.

Today's Reading: Beginning with this chapter, we will examine ourselves anew. "Lessening the Self" is exactly what it says it is. God is not made greater as we lessen ourselves, but we grow in our lessening and become more precious by what we are not.

Questions: Taken from the reading, complete the following sentences with a short answer.

1. Refrain _____ any of those things that could be less than God.
2. Lose such thoughts completely in that _____.
3. You need to forget _____ other than yourself.
4. Love the self, but also _____ for the sake of that very thing loved most.
5. Driving those things away until _____.
6. Even hate to think of yourself when you realize that this _____.
7. Allow sin to remain and it would reside _____ and your God.
8. _____ who must break away from all thinking and feeling.
9. When you have forgotten all …, you have forgotten _____.

Discussion Questions:

10. "Despise what you are, not who you are." The world would have you believe the opposite, to love the "what" you are but not the "who" you are. God loves the "who" of all who love him. **Discuss the difference between "what" and "who" and ponder these words.**

11. The opening paragraph again reminds us that the Cloud of Forgetting has, as its purpose, a place for our shelter and growth. This is where we now dwell, a plateau that is neither of the earth nor of heaven, but between, ready to rise to one and eager to forget the other. **Consider this plateau where we dwell, reminding ourselves what a wonderful gift from God it is.**

12. Lest we forget, the good monk once again reminds us that we are "a foul and stinking lump" and that our "self is sinful." We may not be readily willing to express that truth to others, but by now I assume we're aware there is more than a little truth in what he says. Then he adds, "This lump of sin is nothing other than yourself." In conclusion, he said, "It [sin] desires to remain within you; it has no desire to depart from you." **How can we limit the effect of the sin that is within us when it clings so tenaciously?**

Final Word: Trust the word of one who is an addict; evil has great talons that it has plunged into my flesh and I cannot break free from its clasp. It is a lusting pain I will take with me to my death, but not beyond! I desire drink; I over-eat, etc. To call my flesh a "lump of sin" is using kinder words than I feel toward it. In this, the monk and I are of one mind. This book we are reading has changed my life. May it be so with you.

The Cloud of Unknowing   CHAPTER FORTY-FOUR: Love and Sorrow (115-7)

Review: Forgetting ourselves is one of the greatest gifts we might find in the Cloud of Forgetting. It is a shelter from the sins of the world, yet when we enter we bring our own sins with us, inescapable like an incurable disease. It is ever corrupting, but then we find Grace and with that Grace learn that with long therapy, great sacrifice, and effort, we can forget the sin and serve God. The less we are, the better we are.

Today's Reading: In this chapter we read of the depth of sorrow that cleanses the soul of sin and pain, joy that distracts from sorrow, the worthiness of God, and we end with the perfect love of God. This is a chapter worth reading!

Questions: Taken from the reading, complete the following sentences with a short answer.

1. The destruction [of these thoughts] would make you _____.
2. This grace requires nothing more than a _____.
3. This is true sorrow; this is a perfect expression of _____.
4. Those who feel it deeply are those who know _____.
5. Sorrow cleanses the soul not only of sin, but _____.
6. _____ a soul from thinking and feeling its sadness.
7. The soul is _____ in return for its righteous workings.
8. Here God is well pleased, for then we are _____.
9. All that is truly desired is to _____ about one's own existence.

Discussion Questions:

10. The book says "strong and deep spiritual sorrow" (p. 115) is required to appreciate the Grace granted us. Sorrow is one of the building blocks to rebuild our lives; eventually it leads to joy. **Spiritually speaking, what role did sorrow play in your life? Did it deepen you?**
11. We are asked to sit still. It sounds easy but it's not. The monk said we ought to sit "as if you were in a deep sleep, exhausted from your weeping, sunk deeply in your sorrow." This is a moment of total surrender, vulnerable to the world as you feel your own sadness. I can imagine this in a darkened room with a single candle, silence around you, and sorrow within. The goal is to know yourself better. **Why would the monk want you to face your sorrows?**
12. The ultimate goal in this exercise of sorrow is "to stop thinking and feeling about one's own existence" (p. 117). It is as if we lived in a forest of sorrows and memories, but God wants us out in the meadow. **If we took this radical step, who do you think you would meet in the meadow?**

Final Word: Tall buildings are built by first digging down deep. A good foundation tells you how high the building can go. Sorrow is the name of our personal foundation; at the bottom when you hit bedrock, you find joy. Then you can start building. Build tall, strong, and straight, my friend.

The Cloud of Unknowing   CHAPTER FORTY-FIVE: Falseness (118-120)

Review: In the second chapter of the "Lessening the Self" section of the book, we looked at the role of sorrow in self-examination. This is the pain and sadness that leads to joy and comfort by making ourselves more vulnerable. The summary line would be: "Stop thinking and feeling about one's own existence." The reward for sorrow turns out to be love. Not bad!

Today's Reading: You are no longer a rookie. The monk has declared that anyone who has read this far into the book is probably ready for the full message. Chapter 45 tells us to be aware of either misleading or being misled by cunningly devised temptations that hide themselves in any pride we feel.

Questions: Taken from the reading, complete the following sentences with a short answer.

1. Unless and until one has endured trials, one can be _____.
2. All these troubles are the result of the desires of _____.
3. As their _____, they begin to conceive that these words aren't spiritual.
4. In a short time they fall out of _____.
5. Snared by their spiritual blindness and inflamed flesh, victims of _____.
6. _____ is too often only a feigned fleshly nature and not spiritual.
7. In truth, the _____ is caused by their own pride.
8. There comes a false knowing that is from _____.
9. You must be wary in all your labors, for you _____.

Discussion Questions:

10. To be victims of our own temperament is a terrible indictment of the behavior we often show to others. We must never rage or rail against others; and yet events occur that might enrage us; and still we must not rage against others who are also loved by God. **Offer any personal insight or incident that you are aware of that relates to your unique temperament. Do you try to keep your real temperament hidden? Why?**
11. Likewise, the falseness of our pride has often left us in vulnerable or humorous situations, times when it would have been better to surrender to the truth rather than demand our own way. Pride is a form of pretense that keeps us from the truth. **What is so alluring about the temptations of pride that it seems to prefer vanity to the truth?**
12. The monk again refers to the devil, here calling him a "fiend." He believed in the very real presence of evil and the devil in his world. It isn't a bad thing to consider a personification of evil, the person or the thing that tempts us to do what is wrong or unhealthy. **Discuss your thoughts of Satan, the devil, or the fiend spoken of here.**

Final Word: The lie seems to be so much more attractive than the truth. That which is false can be claimed without the effort that the truth demands. Our pride and vanity make us vulnerable to lies; knowingly and wistfully we opt for what is wrong. Our 700-year-old monk friend wishes us to avoid all those falsehoods. We need more friends like him.

The Cloud of Unknowing   CHAPTER FORTY-SIX: Heed Not Your Own Heart (121-2)

Review: These are key words from Chapter 45: deceived, pride, flesh, worries, temperament, falseness, troubles, *et al*. It's a chapter dedicated to causing us to be more careful, to examine ourselves and our motives, and be forever wary. It was not a pleasant chapter, but we know the truth never is. Be ye wary in all your labors.

Today's Reading: Today's reading is entitled "Heed not your own heart." What a sad thought. Yet it is good advice, for truly we are most vulnerable in our hearts. Be vigilant and let your spirit find peace in the final paragraph of the chapter.

Questions: Taken from the reading, complete the following sentences with a short answer.

1. For your sake and for the sake of God's love, _____.
2. Work more with _____ than with _____.
3. Fleshly ways of the body's desires, but these feelings are _____.
4. Festering pain that was begun as _____.
5. _____ as if you were a greedy greyhound.
6. A greedy greyhound pretending to suffer with a _____.
7. Refrain from listening to the _____.
8. There is wisdom ... to keep from God the depth _____.
9. Find joy in this playful work with God that the _____.

Discussion Questions:

10. This book is a guidebook to lead you closer to God. Have you ever felt mocked by those of the world for trying to live the Christian life? **How did you handle it?**
11. In the last chapter we spoke of the devil. Here we have a wonderful alliteration, a "fantasy feigned by fiends" (p. 121). **Is the devil a fiend or is he more subtle? Try to describe him according to the monk's thinking.**
12. This question is from the book, not the chapter. Many readers are weary of the readings, being constantly reminded of our shortcomings, already assured of our innate sinfulness. It gets depressing. But the journey is never easy. The Holy Spirit is with those who read these ancient words (and those who do not). Trust that Spirit. Growth happens. **Share with others some of your feelings caused by this book so far.**

Final Word: Sometimes I think I have found the place where the devil dwells, and it is in my heart. I hate that, I hate thinking that, I hate telling you that; all these three "hates" are part of the proof. Yet, within me is also an even stronger spirit that is not of the heart or the mind, it is a place of peace wherein the Spirit dwells.

The Cloud of Unknowing   CHAPTER FORTY-SEVEN: Things Kept from God (123-5)

Review: Savor the things of God. Do not speed-read here; wallow in the message. Consider this reading to be a source of joy. Chuckle on occasion, and as the final image of Chapter 46 tries to portray, consider God as a parent who loves you beyond all doubt, holding you close. Imagine yourself as the Teddy Bear to whom the two-year-old clings. You are being held.

Today's Reading: Chapter 47 begins with providing the image of being loved, and then bursts with joy. It tells us to keep our passion for God unmentioned; then it tells us to live out that joy with assurance of God's presence in our lives.

Questions: Taken from the reading, complete the following sentences with a short answer.

1. Bring yourself away from _____ that your fleshly feelings might lead you.
2. _____ are things that lead us further from God.
3. We stress and strain ourselves in trying to live both _____.
4. _____ from God, it is wrong.
5. _____, concealing the very stirrings of your desire of God.
6. The more your spirit _____, the less it has of the flesh and is nearer to God.
7. God's wisdom and eyesight is _____.
8. God is in the purity of spirit because _____.
9. Comprehend this: a spiritual thing is as if it were a _____.

Discussion Questions:

10. When we think of things we wish we could keep from God, they tend to be negative things. Here is an opposite suggestion, and I restate it as: Do not allow our passion for God to interfere with our service to God. Truly, there are some people so devout about being a Christian that they seldom behave like Christians. **How do we keep a balance here?**
11. Do not playfully hide your love for God lest you show the behavior of a fool. There are situations when we could kid someone about our faith rather than admit and testify to the depth of our faith. It can seem like the easiest thing to do at the moment, but it is not the best answer. **Share any circumstances where you ought to have been quiet or where you ought to have spoken out about your faith.**
12. God is a Spirit—but we all have an image of God. If you were to ask me, I would say I hope God smells like a mango: this is a silly image and yet it brings me joy. How do you visualize God? Because God is Spirit, there can be no wrong answers, for God will appear as God and nothing else. **Describe your image of God.**

Final Word: Our faith is our shield; it is with us always, yet it is not used unless there is a need to help others. Doing what is good and right is good, as we should do often, yet without necessarily flashing our faith like a badge. Let others see our faith through our actions; let them ask about it. Strive to be open and honest, knowing we are divinely armed.

The Cloud of Unknowing   CHAPTER FORTY-EIGHT: Thoughts (126-8)

Review: Chapter 47 was both complex and simple. It was designed to push us in our faith and understanding of our relationship with God. Here is a summary of a few phrases: hide your deep desires away from "reckless ways," "childlike", "spiritually," etc. The key comes from the first paragraph, "If you were not told, [it] might cause you to wrestle for a long time before you began to understand them." Consider reading Chapter 47 again, aloud and joyfully.

Today's Reading: This chapter reaches inside us and examines our thoughts. It tells us to keep working, speak well, and discriminate with each of our thoughts, examining ourselves to always seek what is good and Godly. If you have trouble discerning what is right, the book urges you to give your thoughts a "full and careful examination." Take your worries to the Holy Spirit or, if you have one, a discreet mentor or advisor.

Questions: Taken from the reading, complete the following sentences with a short answer.

1. You should never cease _____.
2. I urge you to _____ as you feel yourself led to speak.
3. God will _____ what God will.
4. These rewards come from _____, from within that blessed servant.
5. Desires of your fleshly heart; you must _____.
6. It's proper for us to always be far from _____ that might easily beguile us.
7. _____, do not push yourself to find wisdom in this world.
8. _____ the stirring of your heart concerning those graces.
9. Certified by the Spirit of God or else judged by the counsel of _____.

Discussion Questions:

10. "God will do what God will do." That is a quotation from the book. Sometimes people imply that if you live your life with exact correctness and ask nicely, God will grant all your wishes. These two outlooks are opposite. **Explain which of these two perspectives you agree with more.**

11. Look up the word "discriminate" in the dictionary. We use the second definition, the ability to discern the differences in something. We are told to "discriminate," deciding between good or evil. But it is only ourselves, our actions, and our thoughts that we can really evaluate. It is not only the devil, others, temptations, but it is we who can lead ourselves astray. Discriminate regarding yourself, but not others. **Discuss how hard this can be.**

12. A "discreet mentor" is hard to find and should be treasured. When you need help or a comforting word, is there anyone you turn to for wisdom and guidance? **Describe those qualities of the person whose judgment you trust.**

Final Word: Some of the ministry we are called upon to do is to be that "discreet mentor" to others. Pastors, preachers, priests and teachers are mentors, often only in a minor way. But to be a spiritual advisor requires every spiritual aspect to align with the ways of God, to listen and to heed the Spirit. If you take that role upon yourself, be continually in search of the spirit within yourself in order to guide others.

The Cloud of Unknowing   CHAPTER FORTY-NINE: Perfection of Will (129-130)

Review: Chapter 48 was really about control. It was about our being careful, in knowing ourselves, and doing what is right. The word "discriminate" has picked up a truly ignobly modern connotation, but the ability to evaluate yourself is a good thing. It is the negatively social use of the noun "discrimination" which we must avoid. That's not what that chapter was about.

Today's Reading: A short chapter, the author lures us with the perfect bait, "Perfection of Will." The chapter urges us to pursue love and find joy. In our limited world, our good will is the only substance of perfection we can achieve. Any spiritual perfection we would find in life can only be found in searching for a way to be closer to God, but it is never perfection.

Questions: Taken from the reading, complete the following sentences with a short answer.

1. Lean upon that meek stirring of love that is in your heart and _____.
2. This will be your _____ and bring you to a spiritual joy in life.
3. It is _____ for all that God does.
4. This is the _____ that is the substance of perfection.
5. Nothing else can hamper this good will. The world calls them _____.
6. In heaven they will be united with that _____ without fail.
7. The substance of them here (on earth) is only a _____.
8. There can be no _____ that can appeal to anyone here.
9. _____ for the sake of God's will.

Discussion Questions:

10. When it comes to things of God, as humans we limit God by our vocabulary. For us to seek perfection in this world would be to mock God, who alone is perfect. Our form of perfection is mockery. God's standard of perfection is not ours to understand. **Discuss both the monk's and your understanding of the word "perfection" and how it applies to our worship of God.**
11. If we can't be perfect, what can we be? There are two distinct answers to this question: the world's view and the Contemplatives' view. **Define and compare these two concepts of perfection.**
12. From p. 130, "When one feels the perfection of will" that one does not speak of our "perfection" but of the feel of perfection. Perfection is like the wind; you can feel the wind, but you cannot be the wind. Real perfection is the sure knowledge of the things divine, a quality possessed by God alone. Perfection is not a state for us, but it can be our focus. **How might we release ourselves from the desire to be Perfect?**

Final Word: If we were "perfect," we'd never know it because our quest is not for perfection but for the ways of God such as we can only find in the Cloud of Unknowing. Those who might dare to judge anything about us as being perfect will always be wrong. For without God, there is no perfection and no way to judge it. If perfection were to be found in us, it would be God they saw, not us!

Adding here a point of nonsense, I tell my friends that I expect them to be as perfect as I am, and then I laugh. For some reason I don't understand, I never laugh as hard as they do.

The Cloud of Unknowing   CHAPTER FIFTY: Both the Weak and Strong (131-2)

Review: Perfect is that state in which God exists. He does not dwell there; he is that state. To struggle in this world for perfection is a wasted effort. To be at peace about not being perfect is a part of God's gift to us. It isn't perfection God seeks in us; it's our passion, our awareness, and our faith.

Today's Reading: God judges every case and individual according to his/her strengths and the Grace God grants. All gifts are not the same; some have more comfort and others have more tribulations—yet all who come are cleansed fully and graciously. It is not for us to judge what others have, but to move in our confidence in God and tend to our own calling.

Questions: Taken from the reading, complete the following sentences with a short answer.

1. You should direct all your focus toward _____.
2. Body or spirit, may they never be treated as more _____.
3. We ought to treat all else [that is not love] with a _____.
4. As these other things come, welcome them; but _____.
5. Beware so you are not stirred to love God for _____.
6. All these things are in accordance to the _____.
7. These the Lord will cleanse them _____ with sweet comforting.
8. Being strong in spirit, [some] can find their own comforts _____.
9. These are they who do not need to be _____.

Discussion Questions:

10. Indifference used to mean that someone didn't care about issues for which others were passionate. Then we read that our love of God should be our only focus and we ought to treat everything else with a sense of indifference. It turns out it doesn't mean we don't care about issues, only that nothing but "God alone" can demand our attention. **Should this be true?**
11. To look with indifference at your neighbors' apparent success of bigger, more, and newer things than what you have can be difficult. We who seek after the things of God do not necessarily choose poverty and simplicity as a way of life, but we do need to be indifferent to the things others around us have. **How have you coped with doing what is right and yet remained indifferent to others' apparent success and possessions?**
12. Meekness remains a difficult thing to define. It's probably easier to offer an illustration than to try to put it into words. **In your own words, observations, and examples, define meekness in what you have seen in your brothers and sisters of faith.**

Final Word: God does not love according to our strengths or weaknesses, personalities or accomplishments, fitness or beauty, wealth or poverty. Neither do we love God because we have these trivial accessories. Words of comparison do not fit into God's love for us. God sees us each as holy but not holier, dear but not dearer, precious but not more precious than others. The weight of God's justice in judgment is incomprehensible to us; we can only accept that grace in faith, love, and hope. Amen.

The Cloud of Unknowing   CHAPTER FIFTY-ONE: The Lost One (133-5)

Review: I repeat the "Final Word" from the previous chapter: "God does not love according to strengths or weaknesses, personalities or accomplishments, fitness or beauty, wealth or poverty. Neither do we love God for these trivial accessories. The words of comparison do not fit into God's love for us; God sees us each as holy but not holier, dear but not dearer, precious but not more precious. The weight of God's justice in judgment is incomprehensible to us; we can only accept that Grace in faith, love, and hope." Amen!

Today's Reading: This may be the saddest chapter in the book. It starts with a set of warnings of the trials and temptations that might mislead some seekers of God along false, seemingly spiritual paths. The chapter ends with this line: "He never realized that what he thought was for God really had nothing to do with God." This is a good but sad chapter.

Questions: Taken from the reading, complete the following sentences with a short answer.

1. Those things that move your spiritual heart, this is how you find _____.
2. Do not think your own fleshly thoughts and choose to think _____.
3. Temptingly curious and imaginative cravings can _____.
4. [Words]: Hear them in your flesh and not _____.
5. Often there is deceit in _____.
6. With fleshly curiosity for his _____, he misunderstood all the words.
7. With more wisdom than he possessed, he followed _____.
8. He worked in his own way, and in this he never saw _____.
9. What he thought was for God really had _____.

Discussion Questions:

10. The quotation is: "Often there is deceit in the details." Deceit can be small, petty, and hardly noticeable at first, and only in time do you realize it is poisonous. **From your life, relate a story, often humorous, about how little things may have caused you to unexpectedly stumble in your faith walk.**
11. You may be the most dangerous person in your life. I can literally confess my sins but ignore my own confession; I can repent and change nothing. No one lies to me as often and as sincerely as I do to myself. The final four paragraphs in this chapter tell the story of the young disciple who led himself astray. It is a story I can easily identify with. **How do you identify with the young disciple? Do you see yourself or someone you know in that lost soul?**
12. In the story of the lost, young disciple, one who eagerly sought the things of God but soon became his own spiritual guide, we don't know how the story turned out. Certainly he left the order and the monastery; but God doesn't cut us off as quickly as the religious order might. **What would you envision as a good ending for the young man who lost his way to God?**

Final Word: When temptations are so many, so inviting, so certain sounding, it is not easy to walk the good path. This is the name of our good path: "God alone!" You'd think there should be a six-lane, one-way freeway, but it is only that sometimes. God is consistent, we are not—therein lies the problem. I think at the end of our lives the road gets easier to follow, but the thorns and cunningly devised ways to distract us are still many.

The Cloud of Unknowing   **CHAPTER FIFTY-TWO:** Fallen Imagination (136-7)

Review: Some fall away; some stay strong. The path we walk is not easy, convenient, or rewarding in the world's eyes, but to others it is the path to life, meaning, and hope. By God's Grace we move, love, believe, and cherish the journey. Those who fall away often do so when entangled with their own logic. Seek faith not answers, grace and not works.

Today's Reading: This chapter can be read as a "how-to" manual on how to fall away from the path we have chosen to God. Read it as a "how-NOT-to" fall away chapter. It is an interesting chapter.

Questions: Taken from the reading, complete the following sentences with a short answer.

1. _____: this is the main way to madness.
2. [They] read and hear what is said concerning those things _____.
3. They _____ against the course that God would have them follow.
4. _____ will counterfeit some false lights and sounds.
5. _____ will do so until there is only a faint trace of quaint hearing of faith.
6. So filled with falsehood that not even their own _____.
7. That familiar demon finds them weak, who can minister _____.
8. Remember that the evil one does not _____.
9. The devil would not dare to remove _____ completely.

Discussion Questions:

10. Imagination is a poor guide to devotions, especially in times of prayer and meditation. When your thoughts go astray, examine yourself and seek the turning point to understand why your thoughts drift. **Where does your mind tend to go when you enter a period of devotions/meditations?**
11. The devil, the evil one, evil, demons—many theologian-types explain these words away as personification to explain misfortune and superstitions for the timid and the weak. Yet they are words to which we react. Our monk friend certainly believed they were real. **Consider these words and then share what comes to mind when you hear them.**
12. Do you think the devil fears God? Do you fear God? These are personal questions only you can answer, but your answers may help someone else in your group figure out what they fear or should fear. Please share: **Do you think the devil fears God? Do you fear God? Are they different or similar fears?**

Final Word: This chapter is a mirror. It may be the theologically heaviest chapter in the book and yet, for our subject, it is necessary to face. We are vulnerable. We who seek answers are more easily led astray than those who don't care, yet because we care we also become stronger.

The Cloud of Unknowing **CHAPTER FIFTY-THREE:** The Lost Being Lost (138-140)

Review: Chapter 52 was a rock; it was heavy, cold, and did not bounce. If it hit you, it hurt. Worse news, it will continue its theme into the following chapter. Yet underlying it all, through all the wrongs and evils, God's presence is there in the chapter, in our lives, and in all of creation. Do not fear evil, do not mock it, simply continue on in your studies.

Today's Reading: Evil seems to pay rewards. Evil may look elegant, seem good and not wrong. But eventually truth is shown. The deceived find how empty their lives have become. Without substance, tokens of pride and vanity of wit don't serve well at Judgment. God wins. The timid are afraid: the strong wait patiently and confidently and, still, God wins.

Questions: Taken from the reading, complete the following sentences with a short answer.

1. These misled souls seem dignified in their appearances, both _____.
2. Some _____, it is as if there was no spirit in their bodies.
3. Some cry and whine in their throat, yet they are _____ in all they say.
4. They will always maintain their way of _____.
5. People of hidden passions think all they have to do is _____.
6. The devil has ... perfect servants in this life who have been _____.
7. As if they were trying to hear with their tongues and not _____.
8. Being gigglers or foolish jesters or jugglers who _____.
9. Let their behavior be _____ of the one who does them.

Discussion Questions:

10. This is a wonderful chapter. Look at the title of Chapter 53 and expound on its four-word title, "The Lost Being Lost." It is a profoundly simple and simply profound title, telling a very sad story in only four words. **In your own words, retell the story that you found in your reading of this chapter.**
11. Beware of sermons that make you laugh instead of making you think or tremble. When did you last feel repentant after a sermon? A good sermon is one of the few moments each week when we can be exposed to good theology. Thirty-five years ago my brother heard this line, "You are what you read." He said to himself, "My God! I'm the sports page!" He went out that day and changed his life. **If there was a moment like that in your life, please share it with others.**
12. I have heard preachers laughing at their words, "being gigglers or foolish jesters or jugglers who lacked any sense." I have also heard one speak who carved his words in my heart. With that one sentence God used it to began a change in my life and my values. This chapter is a place for the telling of stories. **If you have ever been branded by a single word or thought that changed your life, please share.**

Final Word: Sometimes I think we don't need God to judge us; we have judged ourselves already by our words, actions, thoughts, and intentions. God merely reveals to us those qualities truthfully and lets us judge ourselves. We testify both for and against ourselves. This is probably an oversimplification, but when it comes to things of God, that's the best that I can do.

The Cloud of Unknowing CHAPTER FIFTY-FOUR: The Contemplative's Demeanor (141-3)

Review: The lost are lost because they are lost. They may imitate people of God, speak like us, dress like us, and do everything we do, but they do so in a false image of our faith, for which there is no imitation.

Today's Reading: Chapter 54 is the concluding chapter on the "Lessening the Self" section. The last chapter cautioned us how those of evil often strive to imitate the manner and dress of those of God, often exceeding that image. This chapter speaks of our demeanor, how we ought to behave in the eyes of the world as we struggle to lead holy lives. In this last chapter of this section, we are to look at and continue to examine ourselves.

Questions: Taken from the reading, complete the following sentences with a short answer.

1. Body and soul, making themselves _____ to everyone who might look at us.
2. How to best govern themselves …, for this is the _____.
3. Make all people like them, …, yet they must be without _____.
4. Contemplatives, their manner and their words should be full of _____.
5. Without any falsehood, far from any of the _____.
6. [Be] careful to look like the image of those _____.
7. Unseemly or unsettling words spoken for the sake of appealing _____.
8. Can there be any pride _____ that have been so plentifully spoken?
9. Stench that a hypocrite's words do, prayers that are offered _____.

Discussion Questions:

10. We give speakers an amazing amount of authority to influence our hearts whenever we listen to them. That's what advertisers do, too. Consider who moved you this week with their words and consider how they did it. **What messages have you been listening to?**
11. It sometimes feels as if everyone we meet, every call we get, everyone we see, or every time we open the computer that someone wants something from us. They want to convince us that their cause is the only good one. Too often it's our money they seek, requested in the name of a noble cause. **How do you handle such brash and bold intrusions in your life?**
12. Various deceits please the devil. We must always listen deeply to whatever someone says to you. Then think about their message as you seek for an underlying meaning and motive behind their words, good or bad. For instance, can you recall last Sunday's sermon, what was said and if you found it important or relevant to your situation? **How did it cause you to live differently during the week?**

Final Word: Words are like Christmas wrappings; some are lovely but contain nothing. Some gifts are wrapped in scraps and contain a treasured item from someone who loves you. In the pessimism that is prevalent in today's world, I heard that well-wrapped gifts increase the meaning of the gift and I, one of those pessimists, think that's because today no one expects anything of quality inside. Thus you make the biggest fuss over what you can see. Image is good; it serves a purpose, but it is the content that we seek in life, love, and faith. God probably feels the same.

Section VII: Directions

The Cloud of Unknowing   CHAPTER FIFTY-FIVE: The Deceiver (144-5)

Review: Chapter 54 concluded the individual study, the self-examination. The final installment of that theme encourages us to move gracefully and graciously through life. We must never forget that through our behavior many others will interpret the gospel message.

Today's Reading: The book makes a change of direction here, moving from the individual to a view of direction and manner in which the monk encourages us to move. These eight relatively short chapters are like directions on a compass, opening with the devil and ending with God. That is a good bit of directional advice.

Questions: Taken from the reading, complete the following sentences with a short answer.

1. _____ unwary people in many manners.
2. The devil does not have to tempt them with things _____.
3. He (the devil) makes them behave like those _____.
4. _____, for it is only the fires of hell welling within their brains.
5. The devil is a _____ no more a worldly body than an angel has.
6. The devil's appearance is always in _____ to those he seeks.
7. The image within his form shows his servants _____.
8. Without discretion, suddenly _____.
9. One must have _____, able to discern between good and evil.

Discussion Questions:

10. We can be tempted by things that look good and right—yet turn out so very wrong. Do you have a personal example of this, when what seemed so right ended badly? **Staying within your comfort zone, please share a story or two. Be assured, we all have them.**

11. Sin so often looks, tastes, and smells more alluring than godly things. This is the nature of sin, to be bold and tempting. Faithfulness is even more bold and alluring for those who know and seek God, but the world can't see it. The devil is flashy, but the things of goodness are solid. **How do these descriptions strike you? Are they silly or the truth?**

12. This chapter contains the only words that I purposely deleted because I thought they'd be distracting. I'd hate for anyone to recall only this single paragraph from the entire book. You can find the deleted 182-word section on page 196 of the accompanying text. Without any proof, I suspect that a later copyist added his own thoughts. **Discuss the deleted paragraph as time allows.**

Final Word: Everything I thought alcohol promised me was a lie. My first drink at 18 told me I was smarter, better looking, more social, and I needed only that magic elixir to be a very charming person. Sixteen years later I was homeless and everything that alcohol promised me was a lie. Alcohol is not sinful; alcohol in me is Sin. I look back and think alcohol was like a beautiful woman who claimed she loved me but took everything I had. I was my own deceiver because I wanted to believe. Genetically, I was born an alcoholic and a sinner.

The Cloud of Unknowing   CHAPTER FIFTY-SIX: The Deceived (146-7)

Review: A deceiver is one who lies to you, misleads you, and generally despises you. I think the devil knows the words of the Bible better than we can ever hope to know them, but he cannot understand them or see God's promise or purpose. Words in him are cold. Where we find life, love, and hope, the devil finds hatred. Satan hates everything we do and are.

Today's Reading: Centuries ago the monk wrote my biography. Maybe he wrote yours, too. This chapter is about the deceived, those who listen and think when they ought to have been believing. It was my story before Christ intervened.

Questions: Taken from the reading, complete the following sentences with a short answer.

1. For things of intelligence and for _____, they choose to leave the church.
2. These [who left the church] rely heavily on _____.
3. In the end they desert and then _____ all the saints, sacraments.
4. They think the statutes of the church are _____.
5. _____ they faithfully choose to maintain.
6. The ones who will not take that _____ way to heaven.
7. Going to hell by _____ instead.
8. The _____, done in secret, will be known.
9. For all their _____, they will be openly known.

Discussion Questions:

10. The previous chapter was about the devil, the deceiver. The devil will forever be a deceiver, but those who are deceived are not necessarily forever deceived. **Share any stories you may have read, heard, or lived when people escaped from deception.**
11. Paragraph 2, line 2: "People choose their own way." That way may be to heaven or the way to hell based not on God's judgment of us, but it is based on the ways we have chosen in life. This is not "works," this is choice. It is only through Christ that we can hope to change our destiny. **Let the discussion of these words begin.**
12. At the moment it may be hard to discern, but the ways to heaven and to hell are actually fairly easy to distinguish one from the other. What you need to do is stop and look around to see what you've done and how you've reacted. The trophies of sin are generally large, shiny, and gaudy; the trophies of a well-spent life are usually toil, sweat, and effort, but they are coated in a layer of love. These are qualities the world seldom admires and never understands. Stop now and examine your life. **Reflect on your life: what trophies do you treasure?**

Final Word: If sin can't buy us with trinkets, vanity is its next bait. When fish take the worm, they seldom think about the hook. As we live our lives, it would be wise to consider the consequences of everything we do. We are so easy to deceive, and yet with God we are less vulnerable to the temptations of the world. Let us be wise: let us trust God.

The Cloud of Unknowing   CHAPTER FIFTY-SEVEN: Up (148-149)

Review: There is the deceiver and the deceived; it is not our choice to be one or the other. Rather, our choice is to be deceived or not be deceived. "People choose their own way," we read in the last chapter.

Today's Reading: Chapter 57 begins with these welcome words: "Let us speak no more of evil things." "Finally," we sigh, eager to move on. Like the legend on a map or the purpose of a compass, we seek direction. This first lesson is simply: "Up."

Questions: Taken from the reading, complete the following sentences with a short answer.

1. Young, presumptuous, spiritual disciples misunderstand the little word _____.
2. The sort of people who make _____ they wish their God to be.
3. They would _____ in clothes and set God on the throne.
4. This is only a _____, although some of it may seem holy.
5. Those who are vulnerable _____ this.
6. Lift our eyes up, heavenwards, as if "up" was the _____.
7. The _____ should neither be directed upwards nor downwards.
8. These specified directions are _____.
9. Actual physical work, which _____ meant for the flesh to manage.

Discussion Questions:

10. In our hearts it is easy to believe "up" is really the way to God, as if it were the only true and holy direction. The monk wants us to know that God is there, but also beside us, in front and behind us, beneath and within (in all aspects). The lesson is this: Don't limit God. **Although all answers are probably right, where do you "look" for God to be found?**
11. People are easily misled if they don't think. Our monk friend speaks of the devil who "wonderfully deceived" people to distract them from actively seeking God. **Using his humorous example, in what ways can you relate fly-catching frogs with folks seeming to be holy?**
12. St. Martin (likely St. Martin of Tours 316-397) and St. Stephen (the biblical martyr) are the two mentioned saints who, looking up, saw the Lord Jesus standing in heaven. The monk does not encourage us to look upward, seeking Jesus. **Where does the monk want us to seek Jesus?**

Final Word: The monk is walking a fine line between accepting the Bible fully (as in his dealings with the devil) or not too literally (as St. Stephen looking up at his moment of martyrdom and seeing Christ). In his day, more than a few devotees kept their eyes looking upward, the direction of Christ's Ascension, the direction from which the New Jerusalem will descend, etc. Likewise, St. Martin, on encountering a cold beggar, cut his cloak in half and gave half to the beggar—later, in a vision, looking up, Martin saw Christ in the air wearing his half-cloak. Let us look in all directions for Christ.

The Cloud of Unknowing   CHAPTER FIFTY-EIGHT: Standing in Heaven (150-3)

Review: Which is worth more, the head of the dime or the tail? Likewise, which way is God to be found, only up? We are not to be locked in one manner of devotion, one way in which to serve, one direction in which to seek. Do not, in pettiness, miss the blessings life offers us.

Today's Reading: Chapter 58 is a continuation of the monk's tirade against the error of limiting the directions of God to the directions on earth.

Questions: Taken from the reading, complete the following sentences with a short answer.

1. Whoever clothes a poor man ... they do it unto _____.
2. Understand this: all _____ bear some physical likeness to this life.
3. Let us carefully pick through the rough bark of this issue and _____.
4. We will not feed ourselves of the fruit if _____.
5. Publically kiss the cup, but it is for the wine inside _____.
6. This is not our work on earth, to be always seen _____.
7. We need to know only that He was raised _____ & _____, _____.
8. We must not get _____ issues confused.
9. We are to stand and remain in a state of readiness _____.

Discussion Questions:

10. It was the testimonies of St. Martin (of Tours) and St. Stephen, the Martyr, who our monk claims were the source of the "looking up" theory of bad theology. I hope you did a little extra reading on their lives. Stephen was a martyr; Martin was not. Become inquisitive about the peripheral details of life, do extra reading. **Examine the lives of these two saints.**
11. In the sixth paragraph is the line, "The speaker meant he would stand with his friend, whether the battle was to be waged on horse or on foot." In your life, can you recall a mentor or a friend who stood with you through difficult times? **What were the qualities that enabled them to stand with you?**
12. Tying this chapter into the previous chapter (#57, "Up"), the monk writer cautions us against a rigid interpretation of the Word, here using the example of looking upward for a sign from Jesus. By nature we are vulnerable and weak in many ways. **Name some ways you can protect yourself from heresy entering into your devotion to God.**

Final Word: The reason for this tirade is that the monk does not want to see anyone lose his/her focus on the things of God in exchange for a righteous and religious image of one who seems to be devoted to God. The image they are choosing to serve is false if they choose to look upward. The work of God is real, sometimes exhausting, occasionally unto death. God can use our knowledge of the Gospel to protect us. Be vigilant and study the Word of God.

The Cloud of Unknowing   CHAPTER FIFTY-NINE: On this Earth (154-156)

Review: Two visions are recorded of Jesus standing in heaven, to St. Stephen and St. Martin. What our monk friend is angry about is there are those who play at being Contemplatives, who claim to be as saintly as Stephen and Martin, while demanding the finest cups and eating the daintiest of foods, claiming to be people of vision. They are seen raising their hands toward God, but they are hypocrites. We should never follow their ways.

Today's Reading: If you look at page 7 in the preface of our text, this is the paragraph used to show how this book was translated from Old English to today's English. This chapter, like the last, criticizes those who claim they ascend to heaven based on their own good works. Here such thinking is rebuked rather sharply.

Questions: Taken from the reading, complete the following sentences with a short answer.

1. Regarding the ascension of our Lord Jesus…, it was done _____.
2. Consider those who have set themselves apart to be _____.
3. The real purpose of this book should only be for _____.
4. It is good to gain a full understanding of the meaning of this _____.
5. The perfection of this work is _____ within itself.
6. _____, _____, & _____, these three states need to be forgotten.
7. In this work take no exception to the bodily _____.
8. If you could ascend into heaven in the flesh…, that is something _____.
9. "There is no one who may ascend to heaven, but only _____."

Discussion Questions:

10. Jesus ascended in both body and spirit. There are those of the world who logically figure out that Jesus must have ascended in a new body (false), that our works get us into heaven (no, it's Grace) and that all this religion stuff isn't historical, but mythological (no, no way). Without the ascension of the Christ, we'd have no Holy Spirit. That is why the monk wants to awaken the stirrings in our hearts; it is why he wrote the book. **Why do you think the monk cares about us?**
11. This book is only words written on paper, yet as you read it, you may feel that stirring of the heart. It is not the book that stirs you; it is the Holy Spirit within you that moves you. At other times you may read, say, or pray the words that stir you. **How do you explain such moments?**
12. Three states (time, place, and body) need to be forgotten if you grow in all your spiritual workings. They can steal our attention with cries of urgency or regret. **What is it that distracts you most when you try to be spiritual?**

Final Word: I don't remember what it was like to be without faith. I don't have to pretend to be perfect. I'm a sinner and often a fool, but my faith is the rock to which I cling with joy for being there. It is with horror I think I could slip away. I am one with the monk on this subject. I pray anyone who reads these words feels the same.

The Cloud of Unknowing   CHAPTER SIXTY: Direction of Heaven (157-8)

Review: Our life on this earth has many trials, many of them are self-inflicted. We cripple our spiritual walks with issues of time and place and our bodies. We say things like: "I don't have the time;" "I can't get there from here;" "I'm really not feeling well;" all because it's inconvenient. Don't let those without legs outrun you, those with no voice out-sing you, or the blind better see where the needs are. Mind yourself, limit excuses, and be wise.

Today's Reading: The second paragraph of this chapter, first sentence, contains a simplification of our Christian belief. The point is that heaven is not above us only, despite several references to rising and descending, but above and below, behind and before, to one side and the other. Do not set either limits or directions on heaven or on God.

Questions: Taken from the reading, complete the following sentences with a short answer.

1. Sent the Holy Spirit as (Christ) promised, coming _____ from above.
2. Do not think ... that perhaps you should direct your mind _____.
3. Christ ascended bodily, and thereafter sent _____ in bodily form.
4. Spiritually, heaven is as _____ as it is up, and upward as well as down.
5. Whoever has a true desire to be in heaven, ... such a one is _____.
6. The way to heaven ... not to be accomplished by the simple _____.
7. Our bodies have been presented here in earth, nevertheless yet _____.
8. A soul loves the body and it lives inside the flesh, and thus _____.
9. Our spirit _____ for this time and this place.

Discussion Questions:

10. Terms like "up" and "down" are often idioms, words which, when you think about them, make no sense. "Feeling down, move up, upstart, downtown," etc., don't mean what they say. If you think of heaven being up, would that make you look up physically? Heaven is where God is. **Describe your idea of what you think/hope heaven may be like.**
11. We are truly two: flesh and spirit. The flesh can be cruel to the spirit, but the spirit must love the body as surely as it is commanded by God to love our enemies, our neighbors, and ourselves. **How does your faith cope with those two warring factions within you?**
12. It is the desire of this book to stir you spiritually. The last line in this chapter tells us to be at peace wherever we are. Obviously the good monk never drove in LA or New York traffic. **When you are in a tense situation, how do you remain "content" wherever you are?**

Final Word: Here are two lines from a poem I chanced to read: "The path to heaven is heaven already, / And the path to peace is peace." We overcomplicate our lives and our theology. We hold others to standards we cannot maintain for ourselves. If we could relax and stand in awe of God, accepting his promise without question, we would be more content.

The Cloud of Unknowing   CHAPTER SIXTY-ONE: Spiritually Upright (159-160)

Review: The Chapter 60 was simple: Heaven is found in all directions, not only "up." It ends with these words: Our spirit needs to be content where it is for this time and this place.

Today's Reading: Chapter 61 speaks of the on-going internal conflict between our flesh and our spirit. We are told to be strong and discriminate about our selves and our behavior. Our monk friend tells us to do this thing: to stand spiritually. It is good advice.

Questions: Taken from the reading, complete the following sentences with a short answer.

1. It is good to lift your _____ bodily toward the heavens.
2. All that really matters is that we have been _____.
3. All bodily things are eventually subjected to _____.
4. He returned to His Father even though He was never _____.
5. _____ the body to the spirit, ... is the purpose of this book.
6. The body... seeking any easier way for the _____.
7. We may be the most beautiful things God created, aren't made to _____.
8. We, who stand, _____.
9. Words, by their nature, must always be considered as _____.

Discussion Questions:

10. In the third paragraph, the purpose of the book is restated: "The subjection of the body to the spirit" and "having the spirit lead the body." Earlier the book (p. 155) used the phrase "stirring in your heart" as its purpose. With differing vocabularies but with the same message, the monk tries to tell us to gain spiritual control over our flesh. **How can we help our "intentional spiritual nature" to rule over the desires of the flesh?**

11. We seem tempted to find the easiest way to do almost anything in life, especially the subjection of the flesh. The book warns us to be aware that the easy ways to control our flesh are often shallow and short-termed. Whenever we try to make a change, be it diet or exercise or whatever, we find it is hard. **Why do you think it is so difficult for us to change for the better?**

12. According to the book, words are spoken by the fleshly tongue. Listen to how people express themselves, especially when angry. I might describe someone I was angry with as a "fat, old slob" because I am overweight, aged, and generally sloven in my manner of dressing. I think "dumb" is the most commonly used word of insult. Have you heard or experienced these similar tirades in your life? Do their words describe the accuser? **Please share those stories and observe the similarities.**

Final Word: Chapter 61 ends with: "Those of you with understanding should understand these things spiritually." One of the results of reading this book is I see the world differently now; I understand things differently. Maybe it's more "spiritually." I find I have difficulty explaining my observations to others who do not consider our spiritual nature to be an important attribute. I am always sad when I encounter those moments, but I do not try to correct them. I tell them what I believe; perhaps I casually recommend they read this book if I think they could handle it. Only if they ask me for more do I walk through that gospel door.

The Cloud of Unknowing   CHAPTER SIXTY-TWO: God Is Above You (161-2)

Review: In our internal conflict between the lazy ways of the flesh and the spiritual quest for the divine, we were urged to stand strong, do what is right, and control our flesh (especially the tongue). It is a good though difficult thing we ask ourselves to do.

Today's Reading: Chapter 62 concludes the "Directions" section of the book. I chuckle at this chapter because, having worked too hard to convince us God is around us and that heaven is not only over our heads, the monk concludes by telling us "God is above us." He means this spiritually, not physically, but in our language it could be confusing.

Questions: Taken from the reading, complete the following sentences with a short answer.

1. It is important for you to know the _____ of the words.
2. When [your work] is beyond you, then it is _____ God.
3. All the things of the flesh are _____.
4. The sun and the moon and the stars, ..., are still _____.
5. They [all angels and souls] are, by nature, _____.
6. _____ is found the strength of your soul.
7. Your soul consists of these three main principles: _____, _____, & _____.
8. Your soul consists of these secondary [principles] _____ & _____.
9. After you overcome these spiritual things, your soul can find _____.

Discussion Questions:

10. Concluding this section, this chapter reminds us of where we are. The previous chapter said words of the tongue are flesh. Now we are reminded that the spiritual nature of words is like fleshly/spiritual warfare. Words illustrate the tension. I always thought words are just words; but it is more. **Explain what is meant by "the spiritual meaning of words."**
11. To control your tongue is a challenge. After telling us "speech is a bodily work performed by the tongue," we are then told, "Do not allow words to be taken as evil." We can say "Thanks" and make it sound like an insult. We can say "Really" and make it a question. My wife can say my name with an exclamation mark or a question mark and I can hear the difference. **Do you have stories to share of times when you heard people use kind words as insults or in a mocking manner, whether directed at you or others?**
12. The first half of the final sentence of the chapter says: "It is by the strength of your soul's commitment that the value and the condition of your work will be judged." After reading such a sentence, I long for the simple mantra, "It is by Grace you are saved." I had hoped that was enough, but in the Bible it says, "… the Father, who without respect of persons, judged according to everyone's work" (I Peter 1:17 KJV). **To be judged according to our works, how does that make you feel?**

Final Word: The way we say words can be an indictment or a blessing. I call a really good friend "Chucklehead," an insulting word, but I chose to use it as a term of endearment and he lets me. I can express anger, joy, excitement and political opinions without swearing or being insulting. I try to be careful with words. However, I only use the word "God" in one way and in such a way that it makes me want to drop to my knees. We are known by our words; treat them respectfully.

Section VIII: Mentally Arriving

The Cloud of Unknowing   CHAPTER SIXTY-THREE: Mind and Body (163-4)

Review: Have you been aware that the previous eight chapters have been talking about us, personally? What lies ahead prepares us for work and ministry. The final five chapters are like a commencement speech of caution and congratulations. In this section we need to consider the message as the monk tries to prepare us with as we get ready to face the world.

Today's Reading: These following chapters are lectures, not discussions. When the monk was preparing his first reader, he gave him advice. This is the beginning of the advice; these are not lessons, they are commands. The wise will heed them.

Questions: Taken from the reading, complete the following sentences with a short answer.

1. Your mind is _____ within itself.
2. Properly speaking, your mind does not _____.
3. But the mind does possess _____.
4. Reason and will, its two working strengths, are _____ & _____.
5. The soul cannot be _____, it is not possible.
6. _____ & _____; these two work purely in themselves in all spiritual things.
7. Imagination and sensuality work both _____.
8. Without the help of reason or will, the soul would never _____.
9. Imagination and sensuality are secondary; they are our _____.

Discussion Questions:

10. The opening paragraph of Chapter 63 talks about the fact that our minds have a strength and a power within us. We are empowered by our reason, imagination, will, and sensuality, four strengths by which the monk says we can "contain and comprehend" with our minds. **Explain what he means by this kind of self-control.**
11. Without the help of Reason or Will, the soul would never know its condition, morals, or purpose of life. Two sentences earlier he wrote, "The two principal working strengths are Reason and Will; and these two work purely in themselves in all spiritual things." **What is your understanding of what the monk is telling us?**
12. Our Imagination and Sensuality are called "secondary" workings of our mind. Apparently this conclusion was reached because they are considered to be elements of the flesh and not of the spirit. These "workings" are more vulnerable to sin than are Reason and Will. **In what ways can our imagination contribute to our on-going sinfulness?**

Final Word: Did you notice in our reading that reason, will, imagination, and sensuality are our "fleshly instruments?" They are our "five wits." Some translators say the five must be referring to the five senses of the bodies; I prefer to think our good monk added one and one and one and one and got five, the math of a theologian. It is like "trinity thinking," where three are one. Do not be troubled.

The Cloud of Unknowing   CHAPTER SIXTY-FOUR: Reason (165-6)

Review: Our introduction is a mental examination being described in this Section. The mind is seen as being divided into Reason and Will, representing the Spirit. Imagination and Sensuality are seen as fleshly instruments. It is an oversimplification and yet it works to define how we operate in the world. It's as true today as it was in the 14th century.

Today's Reading: "Reason" is defined, according to Wikipedia, as the power of the mind to think, understand, and form judgments by a process of logic. It's a very modern definition. The monk defines it as the ability to know good from evil. In today's world, it is much less of a spiritual definition of a word. Alas.

Questions: Taken from the reading, complete the following sentences with a short answer.

1. Reason is the _____ by which we are able to divide that which is good or evil.
2. Evil comes from ____, good from ____, worse from ____ and better from ____.
3. But now Reason has become so _____ it can no longer labor at this work.
4. _____ through which we choose what is good.
5. Good [is chosen] only after its state is determined by _____.
6. Before sin entered the world, it was _____ that guided our choices.
7. Will now can savor a thing, _____ when, in truth, [it] is evil.
8. A thing is fully evil, even though it bears the _____.
9. Will and the thing that it desires are found in a mind that tries to _____.

Discussion Questions:

10. According to theologians, Original Sin never gave us a chance to be perfect. Yet, according to the monk, it is toward that Perfection that we begin our ascent into the Cloud of Unknowing where God dwells. These are amazing concepts. **Is sin found in a newborn infant or would you say sin enters our flesh later? Which do you say is true? Why?**
11. Reason can be either good or bad according to the way people use it. We can apply reason many ways; it can be either a selfish rationalization or a confession. Perhaps it is a wall by which we surround ourselves to protect us from the world. Reason is a tool. **How do you use your "reason" in your life, as opening yourself to the world or as a self-defense?**
12. This Strength we are talking about is not Will, but it is that "strength of character" by which we can discern the difference between what is good, better, or best for ourselves. Our Strength of Character both guides and limits us. **Describe your "Strength of Character?"**

Final Word: These chapters are for thinking. These four chapters, Mind and Body, Reason, Imagination, and Sensuality, have this as a goal: to know the world and ourselves better. They paint a big picture with the hope we can better understand our history, our place in this world, and what it is we hope to find when God, who has never lost us, finds us in the Cloud. Consider these chapters as they apply to you. There is richness there. As Chapter 63 said in the end: "There is truth in this."

The Cloud of Unknowing   CHAPTER SIXTY-FIVE: Imagination (167-8)

Review: Strength, Reason, and Will are some of the elements we needed to survive the impact of Original Sin on our lives. We have spoken more of ourselves than of God in this current section. That will change later. For the sake of these lessons, remove the haste from your life and slowly consider who you are and how you got here, savoring the time/journey.

Today's Reading: To study imagination is like getting a flu shot: most return healthier, some get sick from the injection. When we handle imagination, it can be dangerous—like handling a live virus. But it is an issue we must face. Apparently, now is the moment.

Questions: Taken from the reading, complete the following sentences with a short answer.

1. Imagination is that power through which we _____.
2. Imagination and those things that work in it are _____.
3. Before sin entered the world, Imagination was obedient to _____.
4. Now _____ is no longer restrained by Reason or by the light of Grace.
5. It is the nature of sin to be _____.
6. These [sinful] images are always _____.
7. Contemplatives come to seriously consider _____.
8. [Contemplatives] understand themselves better when imagination _____.
9. These images are a form of disobedience, they are the result of _____.

Discussion Questions:

10. We read: "Imagination is a power." Identify some of the creative thoughts that can begin as good thoughts but soon start to twist, as if they turned evil before we could consider their potential outcomes. **Evaluate the dangers and blessings of our imaginations.**

11. In the second paragraph, we find a poignant phrase, "Conceits of the flesh." Here is the most painful example I can imagine to illustrate this idea: Watch people look at themselves in a mirror. Then, even worse, look at yourself closely. Consider yourself at that moment. Do you see only flaws or can you see that soul within you, the part of you God loves deeply? Faith in God also includes belief in oneself. **Who do you see when you look in the mirror?**

12. Wretchedness is a gift. Wretchedness is the quality of being honest with oneself. Wretchedness leads to meekness, which is the reason why Contemplatives must face their own wretchedness and limitations. **How can we come to terms with our wretched state?**

Final Word: I am wonderfully, deeply, and painfully wretched and I think it's funny! How could anyone turn out like I did? My path has been fraught with trials. I've come up short on very test or trial given me. Sometimes I fail completely; worse is that sometimes I think I almost passed when, in truth, I never came close. Why do I think it's funny that I'm so hapless? It's funny because God, with a heart I cannot begin to comprehend, loves me for the way I am. I am like a quadriplegic trying to climb a mountain; it's not the conquest God seeks, it's the effort.

The Cloud of Unknowing   CHAPTER SIXTY-SIX: Sensuality (169-170)

Review: Imagination without vanity is inconceivable. Yet the chapter said that the imagination shows the real self, very important to the Contemplative. Imagination was greatly affected by the Fall; it moved from being under Reason to being under the Flesh.

Today's Reading: Sensuality has two purposes, to serve the needs of the body and to serve the lusts of the flesh. The Will once ruled sensuality; under the influence of Original Sin, it has become a strain on us.

Questions: Taken from the reading, complete the following sentences with a short answer.

1. Sensuality is a power in our soul that _____ itself through the senses.
2. Sensuality has two parts, one that addresses the _____, the other _____.
3. [Sensuality] stirs us to desire _____.
4. Sensuality complains at the lack _____ in delight at their presence.
5. This power and the things that are at work there are also _____.
6. Before humanity sinned there was _____ but it was obedient to the Will.
7. It never provided any _____ regarding either what it liked or disliked.
8. Sensuality is no longer ruled by _____.
9. Sensuality would have our living become more _____.

Discussion Questions:

10. Sensuality is a tool of communication. It is real and it invites a shared response. Our senses feed our sensuality. In itself, it is good—but it can easily be misused. Like everything of the flesh, we need to control it spiritually to be its master and not its servant. What we need to be is a servant to God and master over our flesh. This is a difficult issue: **How do we become the master of our flesh?**
11. For all his words and passion in this chapter, **What do you hear the writer telling us to do with our Sensuality?**
12. Like Reason and Imagination in the previous chapters, Sensuality was once good and controlled by the Reason and Grace. With the Fall, Sensuality was free to run wild with the conceits of the flesh, creating corrupted images. It moved from obedience to the errors of sin. Controlled Sensuality is like a wild horse: if mastered it is beautiful and powerful. **Compare your definition of Sensuality with how our monk friend apparently defines it.**

Final Word: Don't equate Sensuality with sexuality. It is a restless thing, never happy for long. Too often that for which it lusted is soon despised—what isn't easy is to be avoided, and the easy way is the softest way. Flesh complains where the spirit rejoices. Sometimes the flesh is your enemy, but we need it. But, remember, sensuality isn't always sexual.

The Cloud of Unknowing **CHAPTER SIXTY-SEVEN:** Arriving (171-3)

Review: We live in a world abounding in evil and sin. Since the Original Sin, we have been trying to gain control of our Reason, Imagination, Sensuality, and a hundred other desires that run wild within us. The Contemplative has higher expectations of self-control than the average sinner would ever consider.

Today's Reading: In a surprise action, the monk is actually congratulating us for accepting all the hurdles we've had to endure as we continue running to be closer to God and be a better servant of God. Some minor course corrections and reminders are offered; but from the tenor of this chapter, the monk is sure we have chosen the right path. "Then you may truly be in that Cloud of Unknowing," the monk actually tells us. Well done!

Questions: Taken from the reading, complete the following sentences with a short answer.

1. My spiritual friend! Look at the _____ to which we have fallen.
2. When the mind is occupied with anything _____, you'll find yourself bound.
3. When you discover whether you have been _____.
4. Think of the _____, this is proof of the rightful workings of this book.
5. About this time with God, you are no longer two but _____.
6. Do not forget that God _____without beginning.
7. You are something of the nothing _____ spoken of earlier.
8. You can still be a nothing if _____ make yourself available to sin.
9. Behave like a child and both hide and conceal this _____.

Discussion Questions:

10. This chapter invites you to "look within yourself." It is something the world would never encourage but it is part of finding yourself honestly before God. **What are the fears that those who are examining themselves for the first time might expect to encounter?**
11. Never forget that God is God and we are but "lumps of sinful nothingness." God's love gives us our substance, strength, and hope. There is freedom and joy in that sentence. **What would you tell others of the love, wonder, and joy found in this sinful nothingness?**
12. There will be those in our lives who urge us to deny or hide our shortcomings, who encourage you to be who we are not. Being truly honest is something they do not seem to consider. **What would you say to explain our need for honesty, something we do for God alone?**

Final Word: I don't always feel nearer to God. Having examined myself through my actions, words, intentions, and vanities, in other words my "wretchedness," I feel farther from God. I only feel my own lumpiness, my nothing of substance. Strangely, this honesty is a proof that we have, "by God's mercy," "been made one with God in Grace, united with God in spirit, both here and in the bliss of heaven." Really? Really!

The Cloud of Unknowing   CHAPTER SIXTY-EIGHT: Being Nothing (174-5)

Review: Chapter 67, "*Arriving.*" What a strange title. Who is arriving? Is it we who are supposed to be so wretched and vain and sinful because we know we are embarrassed, unworthy, and without merit? Have we arrived? The Grace of God, the Power of the Holy Spirit, and the Glory that is Christ have remolded the lump we are into a vessel acceptable to God. Even as we cry, "No! Not yet!" God, who knows us, embraces us. Really? Really!

Today's Reading: In this section, we are mindful that the monk is defining these things more than he is telling us what we should be doing. Again, this is because he's convinced that we're almost Contemplatives. Let us not prove him wrong, but strive even yet for that high state.

Questions: Taken from the reading, complete the following sentences with a short answer.

1. Learn to fear any _____ in those offered words.
2. Do not go outside yourself, nor be above, nor behind … seeking _____.
3. "Nowhere in the flesh" is "_____."
4. Wherever the work is, that is where you should willfully _____.
5. Where you are in spirit, there you are as certainly to be _____.
6. Only in being "nowhere" will all your worldly thoughts find _____.
7. Let there be nothing but _____ in that nothingness.
8. Let your "nowhere" be your "_____."
9. [Nothingness] is completely _____ to those who glanced at [it.]

Discussion Questions:

10. This is a terrible and yet terribly important chapter. It invites you to be nothing. Seldom in life do your receive such an invitation. Summarize what this chapter says to you and then consider how you might respond to that meaningful invitation. **Please share your thoughts.**
11. To be nowhere in the flesh is to be everywhere in the spirit. "Nowhere" and "nothing" are related concepts, but they are not the same. There is equality in those two states. **Consider both the differences and similarities. Then share your thoughts, as you are comfortable.**
12. "Let this "nowhere" be your "everywhere" and your all; let all the rest be as nothing." This statement will never be understood by the materialistic world in which we live, but in that nothingness peace can be found. **How do you understand what the monk meant with these terms?**

Final Word: I have actually been accused by a number of solid theologians of being "humble" or, as another said, "Sometimes I think you don't have an ego." Seldom have such bright people been so wrong! I am not humble and my ego is so large and strong it's probably not climbable. So I do not listen to their words because they do not know me. I have the image of a simple Christian and that is what they see in me, not the vain man I really am. Yet I am also one who is blessed to be wearing the mantle of God's Grace.

The Cloud of Unknowing   CHAPTER SIXTY-NINE: Nothingness (176-7)

Review: Probably in this world, the perfect state would be "nothing." The world couldn't see you, it would never comprehend what you're doing, and yet God knows, loves, and protects you. Nothing is not what we do; it is who we are. That's amazing!

Today's Reading: If in the last chapter we were being nothing, Chapter 69 gives a place to be nothing. It is called Nothingness and it is a major part of where the monk would have us be. This is one of the more "fun" chapters. Enjoy.

Questions: Taken from the reading, complete the following sentences with a short answer.

1. Our affections can be wonderfully varied regarding _____.
2. Of the flesh and spirit, _____ are depicted here.
3. By hard work and deep sighs with bitter weeping, [our sins] are _____.
4. We hope to reach any state of perfection in _____ from the pain.
5. Unable to bear the pain, they seek refuge in those _____.
6. Those who persevere eventually find some sense of _____.
7. Previously committed sins have been, in the great part, _____.
8. What holds them back, although generally is _____.
9. Only the great _____ remains between themselves and God.

Discussion Questions:

10. Some find terror in nothingness; some find peace. It varies with each of us. But if you find fear, know that peace is near even if it doesn't feel like it. This nothingness is like a blank board upon which God can write a message. Remember that the promises of God always lie ahead of us. **What can you do to help yourself through the doubts and fears that nothingness often brings?**
11. The peace of this world is not being with God, for the Cloud of Unknowing still separates us from God. No matter how great our sense of well being that we are on the right path and at the right time, real Peace is only found in the presence of God. **How does this make you feel?** Comforted? Frustrated? Hopeful? Encouraged?
12. Our ultimate enemy turns out to be neither the devil nor the world: it is we, ourselves. But it is in that nothingness we can hope to find peace. This is a mystery of God. In your life, have you known that peace? **Describe a place or an event where that peace was experienced.**

Final Word: Sometimes when I write, I come to and realize I've been working in a place of nothingness. When I'm with friends and we're talking, there is no time to restrain us; it is a form of nothingness. There is a sense of peace in those moments of nothingness that is delightful, delicious, and assuring. Usually I am alone; if I am not alone I am with people I love. We should learn that when it feels like nothing, it's everything.

The Cloud of Unknowing   CHAPTER SEVENTY: Discernment (178-180)

Review: Nowhere is good, nothing is better. To be nothing in nowhere is delightful. Nothingness may be a taste of eternity, a state of being blessed where the world really can't reach you. God, who is everywhere, is also in that nothingness. There is life in that cloud!

Today's Reading: Chapter 70 concludes Section VIII, "Mentally Arriving." We end it with a chapter on "Discernment." Some might think discernment was an opposite concept of nothingness, but it is not. It is from the state of nothingness that we are able to discern truths most clearly.

Questions: Taken from the reading, complete the following sentences with a short answer.

1. You must work hard to achieve this state of _____.
2. Leaving your _____ is something that makes this work impossible.
3. Leave behind your limited, outward thinking and do not _____.
4. They [the deceived] have naturally ordained themselves _____.
5. In no way will they ever come to the knowledge …, certainly not by _____.
6. _____ happens to our senses spiritually when we struggle to know God.
7. The only true knowing of God is this: _____.
8. A brazen showing their cunning without adding any insight into _____.
9. In the quest for knowledge, let them discern _____.

Discussion Questions:

10. Nothingness could be everything thrown together, or it could be a silent void. Nothing and nowhere is no place in this world. The question is: **How would our monk friend want us to cope with having no control in such a void?**
11. There will be those who will sidle up to you and assure you that you are doing well in God's sight. They will offer to lead you to your just reward. They will laud you for your devoted attention to the things of God. **What criteria could you use to discern who is telling you what to do for right or wrong reasons?**
12. Sounding remotely like some of the Eastern religions, they say things like "Knowing is found only in unknowing." But what they miss is they act as if there were no cloud above them as a ceiling. Christians know it is the Lord of the ultimate Promise who dwells in that Cloud of Unknowing. What those of the East call "enlightenment," we call "Contemplative." What they see as the end, we see as the beginning. **Explain some differences between a Christian's view of nothingness and theirs.**

Final Word: Through our experience with nothingness and nowhere, we are now generally fit to judge, to show discernment, to know the meanings behind their words, and the truth that gives us coherent life. If their words don't lead to God, their words are mockery whether the speaker knows it or not. This is discernment.

Section IX: Example of the Three

The Cloud of Unknowing   CHAPTER SEVENTY-ONE: Aaron's State (181-3)

Review: First you are wretched, then you are nothing, and in Chapter 70 you find yourself capable of judging others by way of discernment. You have become that Contemplative we spoke of many, long pages ago.

Today's Reading: These last five chapters are stories by which we can understand our place in this quest for God. The following stories are given to help us appreciate our new role. Always we need to learn about ourselves before we can know others.

Questions: Taken from the reading, complete the following sentences with a short answer.

1. It is all according to the _____, as God sees fit.
2. According to... the _____ in regard to how Contemplative grace works.
3. Some will never feel the perfection ..., a wonderful feeling that we call _____.
4. Grace of Contemplation can be observed in the example of the _____.
5. A small amount of love has been known to contain all _____.
6. Moses, before he could see this Ark, ... worked in that _____.
7. No one can arrive at the _____ without long travail.
8. Moses did not come to this _____.
9. _____ has been understood by all those who we should wish to emulate.

Discussion Questions:

10. Discernment can be a frightful word. We are told not to judge one another, but discernment is not necessarily a judgment; it can be a reading of the spirit. If you have a child and see a stranger nearby, it isn't doubt you feel; it's discernment. It isn't judgment. **How can we discern someone's intent without making it some kind of judgment?**
11. Although an angry person probably wouldn't believe it, we read that, "a small amount of love has been known to contain all the virtues of one's soul." **In what ways might we explain such a loving sentiment to a non-believer?**
12. "Ecstasy" is a surprising word to find here. As used by our monk, it probably meant "an emotional or religious frenzy or trance-like state, originally involving an experience of mystic self-transcendence," the dictionary's second definition. I prefer the first definition of the word: "an overwhelming feeling of great happiness or joyful excitement." **How else might we describe what the monk is talking about?"**

Final Word: Here and for the next few chapters, the monk assumes we know the Bible stories he is citing. I hope he is right. To understand the scope of God's work on our behalf, knowledge of the Old Testament is important. The more we read the Bible, the more our knowledge will grow. Moses and Aaron and their sister, Mariam, play important parts in the post-Egypt period of Jewish history. You should be familiar with this Exodus story in the Bible (Exodus 2:1 to Deuteronomy 34:12).

The Cloud of Unknowing   **CHAPTER SEVENTY-TWO:** Contemplative States (184-5)

Review: Aaron was the high priest of the Hebrew people after their escape from Egypt. As the high priest, he had the freedom to enter the Holy of Holies where even Moses could not go. Aaron is considered a Contemplative whereas Moses was an Active, thus Aaron could go where Moses could not.

Today's Reading: Some Contemplatives are able to reach a state of ecstasy, sort of a place of divine rapture. These are those who achieve that high state of knowing themselves and are pleasing to God. It is not necessary for all to reach it; Aaron certainly did and even Moses did on rare occasions, according to the monk.

Questions: Taken from the reading, complete the following sentences with a short answer.

1. Contemplatives achieve only after _____ the perfection.
2. [They] feel the perfection of this work _____.
3. Those who achieve this state often find themselves _____.
4. They ... may be tempted to judge others by _____.
5. Some are never able to find this _____ in the first place.
6. They are rare persons who find it easily, rarely does is come _____.
7. They are like Aaron and have access to that _____ whenever they wish.
8. Moses, to whom, at first it seldom came and then not _____.
9. He rightfully feared he might not live to see _____.

Discussion Questions:

10. Those in the Contemplative state find themselves vulnerable, not something they were generally expecting. Yet it is that very vulnerability that makes them most contemplative. **How do we describe this state Contemplatives reach according to what we've read?**
11. It is a bad thing to judge others by your own standards and not the established legal patterns. This is something a Contemplative should never do, for the standards of the world would fall short of the Contemplative's code. Should a Contemplative judge others? **If called upon, what basis might we use to judge others?**
12. We read that Moses went through great trials before he eventually became a Contemplative. If you examine his life, you'd see that time and again he was taken where he did not want to go and did things he did not want to do, including facing God when all others fled. **What traits did Moses have that gave him the strength and courage to do what he did?**

Final Word: There is a hint of elitism in this chapter. It sounds as if some Contemplatives ranked themselves higher than others because they achieved the state of ecstasy more quickly, worked harder to achieve that status, or it came easier. In the middle of the single paragraph, the monk warns, "they may inadvertently be self-deceived," a warning that even at the highest Contemplative state, there are self-induced temptations that can trip us up. We must always be on guard against our own amazingly resilient vanity and foolishness.

The Cloud of Unknowing CHAPTER SEVENTY-THREE: Bezaleel's Role (186-7)

Review: We are all so different, even siblings. Moses fought his whole life to do what God wished; Aaron became the high priest almost without effort. Obviously they spent their entire lives comparing themselves to their brother (and sister). Not only are we different, we are difficult, too. Consider again the Martha/Mary story.

Today's Reading: After looking at Moses and Aaron, now we will consider another: Bezaleel. "Who?" you are likely to ask. Read on.

Questions: Taken from the reading, complete the following sentences with a short answer.

1. Moses _____ how our Lord said it (the Ark) should be built.
2. Bezaleel, _____, wrought the labor and made it in the valley.
3. Sometimes we profit only by _____, then we are likened unto Moses.
4. By our own efforts, helped with grace, and then we are likened to _____.
5. He was the one called on to build it (the Ark) _____.
6. This grace by the teaching of others, … when we have been likened to _____.
7. Oh, _____, look at this work and consider what it means.
8. People doing God's bidding have been thought to be childish by _____.
9. To work in this labor, in this it is for _____.

Discussion Questions:

10. Were you surprised to find Bezaleel's name on the same blessed list with Moses and Aaron? He's mentioned nine times in the Old Testament, six in Exodus. Do not confuse him with the New Testament's Beelzebub, a name for Satan. I love that the one who does actual work is memorialized with his bosses. **Share a time when you did all the work and others got the credit. How did that make you feel?**
11. We read of three very different manners of Grace. Moses, Bezaleel, and Aaron were all Contemplatives, yet their roles seem more like an Active than a Contemplative. God doesn't ask us what we want to be, but calls us for different roles. **Which role have you been called to?**
12. The last paragraph of the chapter begins with lovely words: "Oh, spiritual friend." The monk we've been speaking of turns out to be "our friend, the monk" with whom we shared this journey despite a seven-hundred-year gap in age. To call someone a spiritual friend is a two-way gift. **What criteria do you use to describe someone as a "spiritual friend?"**

Final Word: Dear reader, you don't know me and I don't know you. But we have a mutual friend who has been dead nearly 700 years. He introduced us to each other, and now I would be honored to be considered your "spiritual friend," as you are mine. Thank you for sharing this journey.

The Cloud of Unknowing **CHAPTER SEVENTY-FOUR:** Your Book, Only (188-190)

Review: We cannot escape life without laboring. God takes our talents and multiplies them; each of us has a different calling. As we serve God, we work together. Conflict comes when one tries to direct others in ways not conducive to God. The final words of Chapter 73: "It is God's love that fulfills your part." Your part is part of God's kingdom. Do it well.

Today's Reading: It's OK to walk away from this book and take nothing with you, to never recall it again. Others of us may cherish these words, assurances, and directions as wisdom from a mentor. This book with its wisdom is meant for Contemplatives.

Questions: Taken from the reading, complete the following sentences with a short answer.

1. Leave it now, lay down this book and _____.
2. In this writing he has truly hoped to share some of the writer's _____.
3. We urge you to _____ a second and then a third time, or more.
4. Allow no one else to see this book, unless you find other _____.
5. I pray that you also urge them to _____ as they look this book over.
6. If it is not clearly finished, let them know when they read it may _____.
7. Will be quickly led into error, therefore, we pray, you must do _____.
8. All like manner of pinching souls, I hope they never get _____.
9. This book is not meant for them. It is meant for _____.

Discussion Questions:

10. "If a reader only reads part of the book, then such a reader is lost." This should have been said in the first chapter! They are not "lost," but they may not yet or may never be called to be Contemplatives. That's OK; the world needs more Actives. That may be why it's at the end, so we won't quit. **How did you feel as you read that line?**
11. I love these descriptions: "worldly word janglers, flatterers, blamers, whisperers, critics, talebearers, and all manner of pinching souls." These are titles of those who oppose us as we try to make our lives more of a spiritual walk than how they walk. These are not dangerous people, but they are irritants to God's work. Ignore them, bless them, love them, and do the work. Family members are often the worst. **Relate any stories you might have regarding your encounters with such people.**
12. **What do you do now?**

Final Word: Am I a Contemplative? As was stated before, I wanted to be one, but Africa, that marvelous mentoring continent, showed me otherwise. I teach, I study, I write. I am an Active. So, am I a Contemplative? No. But I love you who are, who strive to be closer to God. In truth, I was called to be an Active. There never was any doubt about that, but it still took me years to accept that calling.

The Cloud of Unknowing   **CHAPTER SEVENTY-FIVE:** A Final Word (191-4)

Review: Are you still reading? I'm glad. Contemplative or Active; Common, Special, Singular, or Perfect; Higher or Lower Degrees, we are family. We live in the Cloud of Forgetting, beneath the Cloud of Unknowing. We are home here. We bless one another. In this, we are blessed. Rejoice, for God is awesome and we honor that.

Today's Reading: After 190 pages, only four more pages remain. Be patient and read them carefully.

Questions: Taken from the reading, complete the following sentences with a short answer.

1. To begin the work of becoming a Contemplative, _____.
2. Such people must know their _____ for things of God are not enough.
3. _____ when it comes, you alone will know if it is truly the work.
4. Before the judgment of the church, _____ the Church's Counsel-Judges say.
5. Either bodily or spiritually, they must _____ first.
6. [Some] thought they'd be able to do what they wished and when, _____.
7. Whenever the feeling of grace is withdrawn, _____.
8. Without error, this call of God to labor in this work _____.
9. So farewell, my _____ friend. We bid you filled with God's blessings.

Discussion Questions:

10. So, **what do you think the odds are that you'll ever read this book again?** When I taught English, I used to tell my students that to know a book they've got to read it three times: the first to learn the story, the second to appreciate what the author did, and a third time for the full meaning of the book to be revealed. In all my years of teaching, I don't know if any of my students ever did as I suggested, but their teacher did. That's the level of commitment when you want to understand what you read. You don't have to read this book again, but please, consider doing so.

Final Word: The author and the transcriber, separated by seven hundred or so years and nearly five thousand miles, are honored you read our words. May God show you the way, unique and meaningful, as you walk through life. This world has changed greatly since this book was first written, but we, as grace-filled Christians, are a constant—sinners in the world and loved, individually, by God. We hope and pray this book has been worthy of the time and attention you gave it.

The date today is:
_____

The journey took _____ days.

THE CLOUD OF UNKNOWING

POSSIBLE ANSWERS FOR SHORT QUESTIONS

These are possible answers to the nine questions in each chapter. There are no "exact" answers, some words are taken directly from the text and others are generalized answers.

    No suggestions are made for Discussions Questions.

Chapter
  1. 1. Common; 2. His precious blood; 3. Special; 4. leave you in the world; 5. Singular; 6. were already through the first two states; 7. essence; 8. perfect; 9. His servant.

  2. 1. dare to think you are; 2. lethargic and wretched existence; 3. Sloth of the world is your enemy; 4. meek and loving; 5. kingdom of heaven; 6. recognizing your many failings; 7. are now your enemies; 8. be afraid to test yourself; 9. does wait for you.

  3. 1. intentional work of the soul; 2. All that is evil; 3. foul both you and your labors; 4. be slow to begin; 5. the Cloud of the Unknowing; 6. remain above you; 7. you want to live; 8. know God and yourself; 9. for you alone.

  4. 1. give an accounting; 2. the strength of your soul / the power of your own will; 3. passion; 4. help of that same grace; 5. totally incomprehensible; 6. never to have sinned; 7. accounting of your time; 8. imagination; 9. Darkness.

  5. 1. The Cloud of the Unknowing; 2. the rest of creation; 3. never distant; 4. deeds / acts done; 5. The Cloud of Forgetting; 6. spiritual things; 7. Cloud of Unknowing; 8. kindness and worthiness; 9. love and praise.

  6. 1. I do not know; 2. The Cloud of Forgetting; 3. the only place; 4. no one can understand God; 5. of the world that you can understand; 6. God will never be understood; 7. never by our thoughts; 8. darkness; 9. withdraw.

  7. 1. It is God I desire; 2. evil will often assure you; 3. but the lies always come later; 4. These thoughts; 5. even as you sought God; 6. Cloud of Forgetting; 7. without any purpose; 8. single word; 9. listen.

  8. 1. is this who urges me in this work; 2. Evil; 3. pleases the devil; 4. Higher degree / a lower one; 5. mercy / charity; 6. above the self although still under God; 7. beneath the Cloud of Unknowing; 8. with love alone; 9. greater error.

9. 1. within yourself; 2. your mind; 3. ignoring these; 4. very private love; 5. The eyes of your soul; 6. vain thoughts; 7. draw you away and hinder you; 8. evil; 9. in God alone.
10. 1. live for; 2. no sin; 3. frail/restrained; 4. pardonable; 5. spiritual heart; 6. Wrath; 7. Sloth; 8. Covetousness; 9. Lechery.
11. 1. thought / reaction; 2. struggle; 3. enduring; 4. reckless consequences; 5. utterly avoided; 6. the disciples (of our Lord's perfection); 7. Recklessness; 8. perfection; 9. suffer and fall.
12. 1. ceasing; 2. Remain forever; 3. evil things lurk; 4. rising and the stirring; 5. stirring of your heart; 6. little or not at all; 7. Virtue; 8. meekness and charity; 9. they do not.
13. 1. God (alone); 2. true knowledge; 3. Filth/wretchedness/frailty; 4. total love and the worthiness; 5. God's worthiness; 6. imperfection; 7. God's desire for us; 8. God; 9. forbid you.
14. 1. true meekness; 2. the truth of the self; 3. foul bodies; 4. holiness; 5. grace; 6. spirit; 7. attained perfect meekness; 8. foul, stinking pride; 9. as much or as deeply.
15. 1. God's grace; 2. great rust; 3. degree of innocence; 4. contrition / confession / atonement; 5. Ordinances of the Holy Church; 6. grace; 7. found them; 8. of those stirred by sin; 9. Gospels.
16. 1. Let no one; 2. have been forgiven you; 3. she loved much; 4. price of becoming a Contemplative; 5. in birth; 6. division between her; 7. sorrow; 8. Cloud of Unknowing; 9. either bodily or spiritually.
17. 1. good and holy; 2. the Active life / Contemplative life; 3. in words too difficult; 4. sweet and pure feeling; 5. contemplation and love; 6. forced to do all work; 7. another work to do; 8. Actives and Contemplatives; 9. Contemplatives / Actives.
18. 1. Actives; 2. let them; 3. complaints; 4. same life; 5. forsake the world; 6. true spiritual counsel; 7. hypocrites and heretics; 8. cease speaking; 9. think no more about them.
19. 1. special saint; 2. no disrespect; 3. time, reason, and manner; 4. lack of knowledge; 5. Mary was occupied; 6. disciple of Christ; 7. does not comprehend; 8. own innumerable faults; 9. We are blessed.
20. 1. must forgive; 2. not listening to her; 3. to rise and help serve; 4. righteous and lawful justice; 5. Martha, Martha; 6. the multiple details; 7. must be loved and praised; 8. never perfectly; 9. but one love.
21. 1. fourth stage; 2. three parts; 3. mercy and of charity; 4. one's wretchedness, Passion of Christ, & joys of heaven; 5. Contemplation; 6. God alone; 7. The first and the second part; 8. third part; 9. Do not meddle.
22. 1. had much love; 2. comforted by the angels; 3. King of angels; 4. seeking him; 5. listens in order to hear; 6. an ordinary sinner; 7. her own sister; 8. Simon the Leper; 9. belong and believe.
23. 1. our love and our life; 2. seek or think things; 3. ought not to speak against; 4. for us; 5. this labor with love; 6. All things necessary; 7. of their faith; 8. height and the worthiness; 9. nothing else in this life.
24. 1. charity; 2. The purpose of charity; 3. God alone; 4. God's will; 5. perfect worker; 6. second, lower branch; 7. work of the truest worker; 8. Everybody; 9. good as possible.

25. 1. special attachment; 2. completely forgotten; 3. True charity; 4. Contemplative; 5. lost through the sin of Adam; 6. its own witness; 7. This work; 8. leave sin and ask for mercy; 9. can comprehend.

26. 1. your own journey; 2. expect trials; 3. the hand of the Almighty God; 4. who is able to do this work; 5. our labor; 6. minor labor; 7. as God likes; 8. no one can take it up; 9. heed that calling.

27. 1. when; 2. what means; 3. what discretion; 4. all who have forsaken the world with a true will; 5. do not seek after the Active life as Martha did; 6. seek after the life that is called a Contemplative life; 7. would labor in the grace; 8. they have been habitual sinners or not.

28. 1. cleansed their conscience; 2. root and the ground of their own sins; 3. Confession; 4. cleansing is in order; 5. be seen and felt; 6. God and the bearer; 7. righteous act; 8. stirred by our own sin; 9. Humanity.

29. 1. who desires to come to that place of cleanliness; 2. labor hard; 3. the greater labor; 4. perfection; 5. merciful miracle; 6. Day of Judgment; 7. Horrible sinners; 8. hell's damned; 9. You dare not judge.

30. 1. given the power and the care over; 2. for a limited time; 3. standards; 4. presume; 5. quickly fall into error; 6. you and your God; 7. spiritual mentor.

31. 1. have done all; 2. you ought to begin to labor; 3. faithful and quick; 4. thoughts and memories; 5. bury these new thoughts; 6. again and again; 7. too difficult; 8. Only God; 9. deeper wisdom.

32. 1. all thoughts of praise of yourself; 2. overlook your thoughts; 3. longing desire for God; 4. an expression of love; 5. cower; 6. surrender yourself; 7. yourself; 8. a wretch and a filthy coward; 9. dry your spiritual eyes.

33. 1. The Burden of Original Sin; 2. grace and the passion; 3. Teaching; 4. pain and embarrassment; 5. personal purgatory; 6. pain of sin; 7. pain from the Original Sin; 8. be afraid of your own failings; 9. inconvenience you.

34. 1. Contemplative; 2. praying & asking Almighty God; 3. any deserving or earning on their part; 4. sinners more often; 5. intentionally or wisely; 6. merciful & mysterious; 7. without grace; 8. the innocent; 9. blasphemy to the gifts; 10. without this grace; 11. to desire more; 12. the laborer & be the sufferer; 13. covetness of knowing; 14. only in the God Who stirs your; 15. not a very subtle devil; 16. that grace.

35. 1. Salvation; 2. Lessons/Meditations/Prayers; 3. open to all; 4. Thinking alone; 5. a mirror; 6. the teachings of others; 7. blinded by its familiarity to sin; 8. No one's thinking; 9. thinking.

36. 1. Sudden insights & blind feelings; 2. your own wretchedness (& of the goodness of God); 3. definitions; 4. manipulate their meanings; 5. deep words beyond your understanding; 6. SIN; 7. than yourself; 8. any fluctuation of countenance; 9. meaningful prayer/thinking

37. 1. grace; 2. to God without any special means; 3. use only a few words; 4. the fewer words; 5. word of one syllable; 6. a single one word of one syllable; 7. a prayer of one little word; 8. emotionally; 9. pierces heaven.

38. 1. height/depth/length/breadth; 2. bogged down; 3. weight of our spirit; 4. a message fit; 5. accordance to this work; 6. Length/Breadth/Height/Depth; 7. the grievous nature of that deep cry; 8. through grace; 9. grace.

39. 1. many words; 2. a word best suited; 3. comprehended in the concept of sin; 4. merely the word; 5. God; 6. two words; 7. seeking better words; 8. True learning and real grace; 9. you are stirred by God to take.

40. 1. spiritual meaning of the word "sin"; 2. wrapped up in one word: sin; 3. great in and of itself; 4. other than yourself; 5. God; 6. no virtue; 7. in cause and in purpose; 8. God alone; 9. God/sin/sin/God.

41. 1. None; 2. discretion; 3. great a burden for you or too little; 4. pains & woes; 5. in all you do; 6. feebleness; 7. God's love govern you; 8. have patience; 9. faithful.

42. 1. get simply; 2. displays of obvious discretion; 3. to perform your labor; 4. have to fight sin; 5. an awakening to finally understand; 6. reckless desire in your eating and drinking; 7. of awakening sin in yourself or in others; 8. its own witness; 9. God/sin.

43. 1. from thinking and feeling; 2. Cloud of Forgetting; 3. everything in God's creation; 4. hate the self; 5. only God remains; 6. self is sinful; 7. between you; 8. You are the one; 9. nothing that was good.

44. 1. vulnerable; 2. strong and deep spiritual sorrow; 3. that sadness; 4. the depth of their own sorrow; 5. also the pain (that has been earned by sin); 6. Joy can distract; 7. not rewarded with comfort; 8. most vulnerable; 9. stop thinking & feeling.

45. 1. easily deceived; 2. pride and flesh and curiosity (of intelligence); 3. curiosity is aroused; 4. faith into worries; 5. the temperament; 6. Their devotion; 7. falseness; 8. the fiend's school; 9. will be assaulted there.

46. 1. be wary; 2. passion/brute strength; 3. dry from not knowing grace; 4. a fantasy feigned by fiends; 5. Grasp not at those things of God; 6. hunger you've never known; 7. crude and the deep stirrings of your spirit; 8. of your desire to please and serve God; 9. world cannot understand.

47. 1. any reckless ways; 2. All things of the flesh; 3. in the spirit and the body (together); 4. Anything that moves us further; 5. Be childish; 6. has spirituality; 7. evermore unchangeable; 8. God is spirit; 9. fleshly thing.

48. 1. your work; 2. speak the good words; 3. do and bid; 4. the windows of our minds; 5. learn to discriminate; 6. any fantasy (of the mind or any false opinion); 7. Do not be hindered; 8. Fulfill the desire and pursue; 9. some discrete mentor.

49. 1. follow after it; 2. guide in life; 3. the joy you feel; 4. good will; 5. accidents; 6. substance of perfection; 7. good spiritual will; 8. other sweetness or comfort; 9. Knowing it is given.

50. 1. the humble stirrings of love; 2. favored or more holy than love; 3. sense of indifference; 4. do not rely on them; 5. the sake of worldly rewards (and comforts); 6. disposition and the ordinances of God; 7. fully and graciously in the same spirit; 8. within their own souls; 9. well fed with sweet comforts.

51. 1. your true will; 2. they are spiritual; 3. lead you to great error; 4. in your spirit; 5. the details; 6. own kindled wit; 7. the pattern of the lost; 8. the devil (was his chief counsel); 9. nothing to do with God.

52. 1. Believe in yourself; 2. they should be leaving behind; 3. unwittingly reverse themselves; 4. The evil one; 5. The devil; 6. vanity can grieve them; 7. vain thoughts to them; 8. hinder himself; 9. the memory of God.

53. 1. in the flesh and in the spirit; 2. pipe emptiness when they try to speak; 3. greedy and hasty; 4. error as righteousness; 5. proclaim the love of God; 6. deceived and infected; 7. with their ears; 8. lacked any sense; 9. the governor.

54. 1. completely and rightly; 2. nature of this virtue; 3. sin themselves; 4. spiritual wisdom; 5. fawning or piping of hypocrites; 6. enwrapped in holiness; 7. only to our wallets; 8. wrapped in meek words (of imagined modesty); 9. with secret pride.
55. 1. The devil deceives; 2. that are obviously evil; 3. self-appointed busybodies; 4. In truth they lie; 5. spirit and he possesses; 6. a form that seems to appeal; 7. the image they desire to see; 8. curious thoughts appear; 9. spiritual discretion.
56. 1. their love of cunningness; 2. their own knowledge; 3. blaspheme; 4. too rigid to be followed; 5. It is these heresies; 6. straight and narrow; 7. the soft and easy way; 8. sins of their foul flesh; 9. false but fair preening in the open.
57. 1. UP; 2. God into the image; 3. clothe their God richly; 4. form of deceit; 5. do not believe; 6. only holy direction; 7. works of our spirit; 8. merely fleshly things to do; 9. is a bodily function.
58. 1. Christ spiritually; 2. revelations; 3. eat of the sweet kernel; 4. we despise the tree; 5. that they truly lust; 6. to be looking up into heaven; 7. body / soul / without separation; 8. physical and spiritual; 9. to help another.
59. 1. in the flesh; 2. spiritual laborers; 3. the awakening of a stirring in your heart; 4. stirring; 5. pure and spiritual; 6. Time/ place / body; 7. ascension of Christ; 8. no one can do but God; 9. the One who descended from heaven.
60. 1. bodily down; 2. upward (during times of your prayer); 3. the Holy Spirit; 4. truly downward; 5. in the spiritual heaven already; 6. walking pace of feet; 7. our living is in heaven; 8. gives it life; 9. needs to be content.
61. 1. your eyes and your hands; 2. stirred by the work of our spirit; 3. spiritual things; 4. absent from the Godhead; 5. The subjection of; 6. sinful sake of its own flesh; 7. serve the earth; 8. stand spiritually; 9. bodily works.
62. 1. spiritual meaning; 2. above you and under; 3. outside of your soul; 4. beneath your soul; 5. your equals; 6. Within your nature; 7. Mind / Reason / Will; 8. Imagination / Sensuality; 9. strength to work.
63. 1. a strength and a power; 2. actually labor; 3. reason and will; 4. imagination / sensuality; 5. divided; 6. Reason / Will; 7. in the flesh; 8. come to know morals; 9. fleshly instruments.
64. 1. strength; 2. worse / better / worst / best; 3. blinded by Original Sin; 4. Will is the strength; 5. Reason; 6. Strength and not Will; 7. thinking it is good; 8. likeness of a good thing; 9. contain and comprehend it.
65. 1. portray all images of things; 2. contained in the mind; 3. Reason; 4. Imagination; 5. active; 6. corrupted and false; 7. their own wretchedness; 8. shows its real self; 9. the pain of Original Sin.
66. 1. reaches out and regenerates; 2. needs of our bodies / lusts (of the body's senses); 3. more than what we truly need; 4. creature comforts and lust; 5. contained in the same mind; 6. Sensuality; 7. spiritual feigning; 8. the grace of the will; 9. animal-like and fleshly.
67. 1. depth of wretchedness; 2. regarding the flesh; 3. straight in yourself and been true to God; 4. very substance of God; 5. have become one in spirit; 6. is God, the God of nature; 7. of substance, the lump; 8. you willfully and with sinful pride; 9. passion for God.

68. 1. deceit or worldly meaning; 2. for answers; 3. everywhere in the spirit; 4. labor in your mind; 5. in your body; 6. nothing on which to feed; 7. diligent labor; 8. everywhere; 9. incomprehensible and dark.

69. 1. spiritual feelings of this nothingness; 2. secret and obscure sin; 3. almost rubbed away; 4. spiritual rest and escape; 5. other bodily comforts; 6. comfort and find some hope; 7. erased through the help of grace; 8. nothing other than themselves; 9. Cloud of Unknowing.

70. 1. nothingness; 2. outward, bodily thinking; 3. labor for these things; 4. to be creatures of knowledge; 5. their works; 6. Assurance; 7. true knowing is found only in the unknowing; 8. the spiritual quest; 9. what they should know and what they should not know.

71. 1. ordinance and disposition; 2. soul of the seeker; 3. ecstasy; 4. Ark of the Testament (of the Old Law); 5. the virtues of one's soul; 6. cloud for six days; 7. perfection of this spiritual work; 8. ecstasy often or easily; 9. Aaron's state.

72. 1. seeing and feeling; 2. through great travail; 3. vulnerable, easily deceived; 4. their own standards; 5. state of ecstasy; 6. easily; 7. inner sanctum; 8. without those great trials (on the Mountain); 9. the manner of the Ark.

73. 1. learned on the mountain; 2. the craftsman; 3. grace; 4. Bezaleel; 5. by his own toil and labor; 6. Aaron; 7. spiritual friend; 8. those without understanding; 9. God's love that fulfills your part.

74. 1. take up another line of work; 2. simple knowledge; 3. read this book over; 4. like-minded searchers for God; 5. take their time; 6. be resolved; 7. as you see right; 8. to see this book; 9. Contemplatives only.

75. 1. be cautious; 2. reasoning alone or hunger; 3. Test this stirring; 4. accept whatever decree; 5. judge themselves; 6. they were wrong; 7. pride is the cause; 8. is real; 9. goodly, ghostly.

Cheater's Guide to **The Cloud of Unknowing:**
(It is with some embarrassment I even suggest this condensed reading.)
Read Chapters **3, 4, 7, 15, 24, 33, 44, 53, 69, & 75.**

Chapters 1-2 divide the Christian world into four groups, the Common (non-committed believers), Special (church attendees but not especially committed), Singular (intentionally living as a Christian), and Perfect (unattainable in this life).

Read Chapters Three and Four

Chapter Three defines the Cloud of Unknowing as the cloud where God dwells, off limits for us now owing to our inherent sinful nature but available by God's Grace after this life. **Chapter Four** differentiates it from the Cloud of Darkness and Cloud of Forgetting. The Cloud of Darkness is where we dwell now. The Cloud of Forgetting is a gift from God, a sheltering place that enables us to focus on God and not on ourselves as the previous chapter had us do.

Chapters 5-6 urge us to stay in the Cloud of Forgetting and accept the fact that you will never understand God. This is a major concession for many people, but it is true for all people.

Read Chapter Seven

Chapter Seven points out ways we distract ourselves with questions, thoughts, and feelings that keep us from focusing upon God! Suggesting a change in lifestyles, we are told to find a single, one-syllable word, often repeated, to keep us focused on what is most important. It's an amulet to bring your mind back to God!

Chapters 8-14 speak of Actives (Christian doers) and Contemplatives (Christian students) and covers our sinful nature, sins, wretchedness and repeatedly shows our shortcomings. The monk urges us to be wretched.

Read Chapter Fifteen

Chapter Fifteen tells us what we need to do to change: Contrition, Confession, and Atonement. This may be the most important chapter in the book.

Chapters 16-23 tell us of the love and conflict between Martha and Mary. They are used as examples to illustrate the problems between Contemplatives and Actives.

Read Chapter Twenty-Four

Chapter Twenty-Four speaks of charity and meekness, wonderful attributes that link us to each other, and urges a family-like relationship with everyone.

Chapters 25-32 speak of the works we need to do, including salvation, judging, and finally realizing we can't do enough to please God. Our solution is to realize our need to surrender our thoughts and selves to God.

Read Chapter Thirty-Three

Chapter Thirty-Three reminds us that we can never escape from our sinful nature. We can live with it only by living for God.

Chapters 34-43 speak of meditation, the focusing our lives, until we finally realize how amazingly inept we are at knowing ourselves.

Read Chapter Forty-Four

Chapter Forty-Four talks of joy and sorrow and how these selfish emotions must be overcome as we move closer to God.

Chapters 45-52 work to convince us of our unworthiness, things the world would not want us to admit.

Read Chapter Fifty-Three

Chapter Fifty-Three tells of how some walk away from this calling and the evil they try to do. It tells of the "Lost Being Lost."

Chapters 54-68 are rules of discipline that are intended to teach us of the dangers and hopes of our mind, especially the role of nothingness we have to master.

Read Chapter Sixty-Nine

Chapter Sixty-Nine gives a place to be nothing. It is called Nothingness and it is a major place where the monk would have us be. In the last paragraph it speaks of that nothing where we are free to be the great emptiness.

Chapters 70-74 are historic examples of people conflicted between Actives and Contemplatives: Moses, Aaron, and Bezaleel.

Read Chapter Seventy-Five

Chapter Seventy-Five is the graduation speech the monk sends us down through the centuries. It reminds us of our promises, our duties, and the trials we will pass through to serve God. Then, like a good teacher, the monk releases us to go and do what is right.

For additional reading, read chapters 1, 2, 5, 6, 8, 9, 10, 11, 12, 13, 14, 16, 17, 18, 19, 20, 21, 22, 23, 25, 26, 27, 28, 29, 30, 31, 32, 34, 35, 36, 37, 38, 39, 40, 41, 42, 43, 45, 46, 47, 48, 49, 50, 51, 52, 54, 55, 56, 57, 58, 59, 60, 61, 62, 63, 64, 65, 66, 67, 68, 70, 71, 72, 73, & 74.

44,000 words

Some Other Books by Marvin Kananen

Jeannmarv's Africa 2013

Jeannmarv's Africa 2015

Walking with Bashō

Jonah: What's Your Whale?

Shadowline

Etta Jones

Making Genesis

Escape from Bondage

The Perfect Planet

Wild Pitches

Raca Roaming

Bad Theology

Made in the USA
Middletown, DE
08 June 2024